THE POWER OF PURPOSE

Setting and Achieving Meaningful Goals Area

Arularase Baskar

ISBN 979-8-89446-849-5

In loving memory of my dear father (Mr Seetha Raman), who resides among the stars in heaven, who may no longer walk beside me but forever remains in the echoes of my heart and the memories we shared. Your wisdom, strength, and the endless love you showered upon me continue to guide my path. Your guidance, love, and wisdom continue to inspire me every day.

This book is dedicated to you, with love reaching beyond the stars, my eternal source of inspiration. May your spirit find comfort in the words within these pages, forever a part of the stories we share."

Whose presence continues to guide and inspire me, even in your physical absence. It was your unwavering belief in my abilities and your constant encouragement that planted the seed of writing within me. Though you're no longer here to witness the fruition of this endeavor, your spirit lives on in every word, every page, and every chapter of this book. Your wisdom, your love, and your memory fuel my pen, as I strive to honor your legacy through the book **"POWER OF PURPOSE"**. This book is dedicated to you, APPA, as a tribute to the profound impact you had on my life and as a testament to the enduring bond between a father and daughter.

To the woman who has been my rock, my mum, Madam Kerushnamal Subramaniam, my guiding light, and my source of unwavering love and support. Your resilience, wisdom, and unconditional love have fueled my passion for writing and guided me through life's twists and turns. This book is a testament to your strength and the profound impact you've had on shaping my dreams. With endless gratitude and love, I dedicate these pages to you, Mom, as a token of appreciation for all that you are and all that you've done.

To my beloved husband, Dr Baskaran Kasi, whose unwavering love, support, and encouragement have been the cornerstone of my writing journey. Your belief in my dreams, your patience during the long hours spent at my desk, and your understanding of my creative process have been my greatest blessings. This book is dedicated to you, my partner in life and in love, as a testament to the strength of our bond and the depth of my gratitude for having you by my side. With all my love, now and always.

To my darling daughter, Ms Komagaal Shree Baskaran, whose bright spirit and boundless curiosity light up my world every day. Your laughter, your love, and your endless questions have inspired me to see the world through fresh eyes and to capture its wonders within these pages. This book is dedicated to you, my little muse, as a token of my love and admiration for the extraordinary person you are becoming. May these words serve as a reminder of the depth of my love for you and the limitless possibilities that await you. With all my heart, now and forever

To my dear brother, Ir Chandrasehgaran Seetha Raman, whose unwavering support, boundless laughter, and steadfast friendship have been a source of strength and inspiration throughout my life. Your resilience, kindness, and unwavering belief in me have fueled my determination and shaped my journey as a writer. This book is dedicated to you, as a token of my deepest gratitude for your presence in my life and the countless ways you've enriched it. May these pages bring you as much joy and inspiration as you have brought to me. With heartfelt appreciation and love, this is for you, my brother.

To my dearest sister, Dr Gouri Baldwin, whose unwavering love, support, and friendship have been a constant source of strength and inspiration. Your laughter, your kindness, and your endless encouragement have guided me through the highs and lows of life's journey. This book is dedicated to you, as a tribute to the bond we share and the profound impact you've had on my life. May these pages serve as a reflection of the love and gratitude I hold for you in my heart. With heartfelt appreciation and admiration, this is for you, my beloved sister

To my wonderful brother-in-law, Dr Timothy Charles Baldwin, whose warmth, humor, and support have brightened my life in countless ways. Your presence in our family has brought joy and camaraderie, and your encouragement has inspired me to pursue my passions wholeheartedly. This book is dedicated to you, as a token of my appreciation for your friendship and the positive impact you've had on my life. May these pages bring you as much joy as you have brought to me. With sincere gratitude and affection, this is for you, my dear brother-in-law.

To my incredible trainers/mentors, especially Encik Zainudin Kadir and Mr Soo Hoo, whose expertise, dedication, and unwavering support have guided me through every step of this journey. Your patience, encouragement, and belief in my abilities have been instrumental in shaping me into the writer I am today. This book is dedicated to you, as a token of my deepest gratitude for your invaluable mentorship and the profound impact you've had on my growth. May these pages serve as a testament to the wisdom you've imparted and the inspiration you've ignited within me. With heartfelt appreciation and admiration, this is for you.

To my cherished friends Mdm Parimala and Mr M.Sivaneswaran, who have stood by my side through the highs and lows of life's journey, who never let me land. Your unwavering support, empathy, and laughter have been my guiding light during the darkest of times and my source of joy during the brightest. This book is dedicated to you, as a testament to the strength of our friendship and the profound impact you've had on my life. May these pages serve as a tribute to our shared experiences and the enduring bond that binds us together. With heartfelt gratitude and love, this is for you.

To my dear known and unknown friends, whose unwavering friendship and support have been a constant source of joy and inspiration in my life. Your laughter, your kindness, and your unwavering belief in me have given me the courage to pursue my dreams and the strength to overcome any obstacle. This book is dedicated to you, my friends, as a token of my gratitude for your presence in my life. May these pages bring you as much joy and inspiration as you have brought to me. With heartfelt appreciation and love, now and always.

Last but not least, not forgotten,
To my divine source of guidance and strength, whose presence has illuminated my path and inspired every word written within these pages. Your boundless love, grace, and wisdom have been my constant companions, guiding me through the darkest of nights and inspiring me to reach for the stars. This book is dedicated to you, my eternal God, as an expression of my deepest reverence and gratitude for your infinite blessings. May its words honor your divine presence and serve as a testament to the profound impact you've had on my life. With unwavering faith and devotion, this is dedicated to you.

If you want to go fast go alone
If you want to go far go together

African Proverb
Martha Goedert.

CONTENTS

PART 1

ABOUT GOAL SETTING

Certainly, let's delve deeper into the topic of goal setting:

Definition: Goal setting is a structured process of identifying specific objectives that you want to achieve in the future. These objectives are typically based on your personal or professional aspirations and are intended to provide direction and motivation for your efforts

PART 2

CONTENTS OF GOAL SETTING

CONTENTS OF GOAL SETTING

The contents of a well-structured goal-setting process typically include several key components that help individuals define, plan, and achieve their objectives effectively. Here are the essential contents of goal setting:

IDENTIFY THE GOAL

Begin by clearly defining what you want to achieve. Be specific about the outcome you desire.

USE SPECIFIC LANGUAGE

Use precise and unambiguous language to describe your goal. Avoid vague or generalized terms.

INCLUDE MEASURABLE ELEMENTS

If applicable, include metrics or criteria that will allow you to measure your progress and determine when the goal has been achieved.

SET A DEADLINE

Specify a timeframe or deadline by which you intend to accomplish the goal. This creates a sense of urgency and helps with time management.

EXPLAIN THE WHY

Provide a brief explanation of why this goal is important to you. What is the underlying motivation or purpose?

MAKE IT REALISTIC

Ensure that the goal is achievable and realistic given your resources and constraints.

CONSIDER THE CONTEXT:

If necessary, include information about the context or circumstances in which the goal will be pursued.

> Here's an example of a clear goal statement:
>
> Vague Goal:
>
> "I want to get in better shape."

CLEAR GOAL STATEMENT:

"I will lose 10 pounds of body weight within the next three months by following a balanced diet and exercising for 30 minutes, five days a week, because I want to improve my overall health and boost my self-confidence

In the clear goal statement, you can see that it specifies the desired outcome (losing 10 pounds), includes a measurable element (within the next three months), provides a clear action plan (balanced diet and exercise routine), explains the motivation (improve health and boost self-confidence), and sets a timeframe (next three months). This level of detail makes the goal statement precise and actionable.

PURPOSE AND MOTIVATION

Explain why the goal is important to you. What motivates you to pursue this objective? A strong sense of purpose can boost your commitment.

Purpose and motivation are essential components of effective goal setting. They provide the "why" behind your goals and serve as the driving force that keeps you committed and focused on achieving your objectives. Here's a closer look at purpose and motivation in the context of goal setting:

1. PURPOSE:

Purpose represents the underlying reason or significance behind your goal. It answers the question, "Why do you want to achieve this goal?" Understanding your purpose is crucial because it gives your goal meaning and direction. Purpose-driven goals are often more compelling and enduring.

How to Identify Your Purpose:

- Reflect on what deeply matters to you and your values.

- Consider how achieving the goal aligns with your long-term aspirations and life vision.

- Think about the positive impact achieving the goal will have on your life or the lives of others.

- Determine what personal or emotional fulfillment the goal will bring.

Example of Purpose:

- Goal: Completing a marathon.

- Purpose: To challenge myself physically and mentally, improve my overall fitness, and gain a sense of personal accomplishment.

2. MOTIVATION:

Motivation is the internal or external drive that propels you toward your goal. It is the energy, enthusiasm, and determination you have to take action and overcome obstacles. Motivation can come from various sources, including intrinsic (internal) motivation and extrinsic (external) motivation

TYPES OF MOTIVATION:

- Intrinsic Motivation: This comes from within and is driven by personal satisfaction, passion, and a genuine interest in the goal itself.

- Extrinsic Motivation: This comes from external factors such as rewards, recognition, or pressure from others. While extrinsic motivation can be effective, it may not be as sustainable as intrinsic motivation.

HOW TO BOOST MOTIVATION:

- Set meaningful and personally relevant goals.

- Visualize your success and imagine how achieving the goal will make you feel.

- Break your goal into smaller, manageable steps to create a sense of progress.

- Find sources of inspiration, whether through role models, success stories, or supportive communities.

- Stay accountable by sharing your goals with others who can encourage and support you.

EXAMPLE OF MOTIVATION:

- Goal: Writing a novel.

- Motivation: Intrinsic motivation driven by a passion for storytelling and a desire to share meaningful stories with readers.

Combining a clear goal statement with a strong sense of purpose and motivation creates a powerful foundation for successful goal attainment. When your goals are aligned with your values and passions and you are genuinely motivated to pursue them, you are more likely to stay committed, overcome challenges, and achieve your desired outcomes.

SMART CRITERIA

- Refine your goal using the SMART criteria:
  - ☐ Specific: Clearly define the goal.
  - ☐ Measurable: Determine how you'll measure progress.
  - ☐ Achievable: Ensure it's realistic and attainable.
  - ☐ Relevant: Align the goal with your values and long-term objectives.
  - ☐ Time-Bound: Set a specific deadline or timeframe for completion.

The SMART criteria are a set of guidelines used to ensure that goals and objectives are well-defined, clear, and actionable. SMART is an acronym that stands for Specific, Measurable, Achievable, Relevant, and Time-bound. When setting goals, applying these criteria can increase your chances of success and help you create clear and effective objectives. Here's a breakdown of each element of the SMART criteria:

SPECIFIC:

- Specific goals are clear and well-defined. They provide a precise description of what you want to achieve.

- Ask yourself: What exactly do I want to accomplish? What are the details of the goal?

Example: Instead of a vague goal like "Get in shape," a specific goal would be "Lose 10 pounds of body weight within three months."

MEASURABLE:

- Measurable goals are quantifiable, allowing you to track your progress and determine when the goal has been achieved.

- Ask yourself: How will I measure my progress? What are the criteria for success

Example: Instead of saying "Exercise more," a measurable goal would be "Exercise for 30 minutes, five days a week."

ACHIEVABLE:

- Achievable goals are realistic and attainable, considering your resources, skills, and constraints. They should challenge you but remain within reach.

- Ask yourself: Is this goal realistically achievable given my current circumstances?

Example: If you currently run for 10 minutes a day, setting a goal to run a marathon next week may not be achievable.

RELEVANT:

- Relevant goals are aligned with your values, long-term objectives, and overall mission. They should be meaningful and have a purpose.

- Ask yourself: Does this goal matter to me? Is it relevant to my life or work?

Example: If your long-term objective is to improve your health, setting a goal to quit smoking is relevant.

TIME-BOUND:

- Time-bound goals have a specific timeframe or deadline for completion. This creates a sense of urgency and helps you prioritize your efforts.

- Ask yourself: When do I want to achieve this goal? What's the deadline?

Example: Instead of saying "Someday, I want to write a book," a time-bound goal would be "Write a 50,000-word novel by the end of the year."

Using the SMART criteria can turn abstract desires into concrete and actionable goals. It forces you to clarify your objectives, measure your progress, ensure feasibility, align with your values, and set a timeframe for completion. This structured approach to goal setting can help you stay focused, motivated, and accountable as you work towards achieving your goals.

ACTION PLAN

Outline the specific actions, tasks, and strategies you need to follow to achieve your goal. Break down the goal into smaller, manageable steps.

An action plan is a critical component of goal setting that outlines the specific steps and tasks you need to take in order to achieve your goals. It serves as a roadmap, helping you stay organized, focused, and accountable throughout the goal pursuit process. Here's how to create an effective action plan for your goals:

BREAK DOWN YOUR GOAL:

- Start by breaking your larger goal into smaller, manageable sub-goals or milestones. These smaller steps make the goal more achievable and less overwhelming.

LIST SPECIFIC TASKS:

- For each sub-goal or milestone, list the specific tasks or actions you need to complete. Be as detailed as possible, outlining what needs to be done.

PRIORITIZE TASKS:

- Determine the order of tasks based on their importance and logical sequence. Identify which tasks should be completed first and which ones can follow.

SET DEADLINES:

- Assign deadlines or target dates for each task. Establishing clear timeframes creates a sense of urgency and helps with time management.

ALLOCATE RESOURCES:

- Identify the resources, tools, and support you'll need to accomplish each task. This may include financial resources, materials, information, or assistance from others.

DELEGATE RESPONSIBILITIES (IF APPLICABLE):

- If your goal involves a team or others who can assist, assign specific responsibilities to individuals or team members. Ensure everyone understands their role.

CREATE A TIMELINE:

- Create a timeline or project schedule that outlines when each task or milestone will be completed. This can be done using a calendar, project management software, or a simple spreadsheet.

MONITOR PROGRESS:

- Regularly review your action plan to track your progress. Check off completed tasks and milestones, and assess whether you are on schedule.

ADJUST AS NECESSARY:

- Be flexible and willing to adapt your action plan if circumstances change or if you encounter unexpected challenges. Adjust deadlines or strategies as needed.

STAY ACCOUNTABLE:

- Share your action plan with someone who can hold you accountable, such as a friend, family member, mentor, or coach. Regular check-ins can help you stay on track.

CELEBRATE MILESTONES:

- Celebrate your achievements and milestones along the way. Recognizing your progress reinforces motivation and provides a sense of accomplishment.

REVIEW AND REVISE:

- Periodically review and revise your action plan as you move closer to your goal. Ensure it remains aligned with your objectives and adapt it as necessary.

STAY FOCUSED:

- Maintain focus on your action plan and avoid distractions. Keep your goal in mind, and remind yourself of your motivation and purpose.

DOCUMENT YOUR PROGRESS:

- Keep a record of your progress, whether through written notes, journaling, or a digital tracking system. This documentation can help you assess your journey and make improvements.

SEEK SUPPORT:

- If you encounter challenges or obstacles, seek support and guidance from mentors, experts, or support groups related to your goal.

An action plan is a dynamic document that evolves as you work toward your goal. It provides structure and guidance, helping you navigate the steps required for success. Regularly revisiting and updating your action plan ensures that it remains relevant and effective in achieving your desired outcomes.

Lesson 5

RESOURCES AND SUPPORT

Identify the resources, tools, and support you'll need to accomplish the goal. This could include financial resources, mentors, information, or skills.

Resources and support play a crucial role in goal setting and achievement. They provide the necessary tools, knowledge, assistance, and motivation to help you reach your objectives. Here are some key aspects of resources and support in the goal-setting process:

FINANCIAL RESOURCES:

- Financial resources are essential for many goals, whether it's starting a business, buying a home, or pursuing higher education.

- Identify the financial resources required to achieve your goal and create a budget or financial plan to ensure you have the necessary funds.

EDUCATIONAL RESOURCES:

- For goals that involve acquiring new knowledge or skills, such as learning a language or obtaining a certification, educational resources are crucial.

- Consider enrolling in courses, workshops, or online classes, and access books, tutorials, and educational websites that can help you learn and grow.

MENTORS AND COACHES:

- Mentors and coaches can provide guidance, expertise, and valuable insights to help you achieve your goals.

- Seek out mentors or coaches who have experience in your area of interest and can offer support, advice, and feedback.

NETWORKING AND CONNECTIONS:

- Building a strong network of contacts and connections can provide opportunities, resources, and valuable information.
- Attend networking events, join professional organizations, and actively engage with others who share your goals or interests.

SUPPORTIVE FRIENDS AND FAMILY:

- The encouragement and emotional support of friends and family can be a powerful motivator.
- Share your goals with loved ones, and let them know how they can support you on your journey.

ACCOUNTABILITY PARTNERS:

- An accountability partner is someone who checks in with you regularly to ensure you're making progress and staying on track.
- Partner with someone who has similar goals, or consider hiring a coach or mentor who can hold you accountable

ONLINE COMMUNITIES AND FORUMS:

- Online communities, forums, and social media groups can connect you with like-minded individuals who can offer advice, share experiences, and provide support.
- Participate in online communities relevant to your goals to gain insights and build a sense of community.

TECHNOLOGY AND TOOLS:

- Technology tools, such as project management software, goal-tracking apps, and productivity tools, can help you stay organized and on top of your tasks.

- Identify and use the technology and tools that best support your specific goals.

HEALTH AND WELLNESS SUPPORT:

- For goals related to health and wellness, consider seeking support from healthcare professionals, nutritionists, personal trainers, or therapists.

- They can provide expert guidance and personalized plans to help you achieve your health-related objectives.

PROFESSIONAL SERVICES:

- Depending on your goals, you may need the services of professionals such as lawyers, accountants, or consultants to help you navigate complex issues or regulations.

SELF-HELP RESOURCES:

- Self-help books, podcasts, articles, and online resources can provide valuable insights, strategies, and motivation for personal growth and development goals.

VOLUNTEER AND COMMUNITY RESOURCES:

- For goals related to community involvement or volunteering, tap into local organizations, nonprofits, and community resources that align with your objectives.

PEER SUPPORT GROUPS:

- Peer support groups are gatherings of individuals facing similar challenges or working toward common goals.

- These groups offer emotional support, a sense of belonging, and the opportunity to share experiences and advice.

When setting and pursuing your goals, it's essential to assess which resources and types of support are most relevant to your specific objectives. Leveraging these resources can make the goal-setting process more effective and increase your chances of achieving your desired outcomes

TIMELINE AND DEADLINE

Assign deadlines or target dates for each step or milestone within your action plan. Creating a timeline helps you stay accountable.

Timelines and deadlines are crucial elements of goal setting as they provide structure, create a sense of urgency, and help you manage your time effectively. By setting specific timeframes for your goals, you can stay focused, measure progress, and increase your chances of achieving your objectives. Here's how to incorporate timelines and deadlines into your goal-setting process:

SET CLEAR TIMEFRAMES:

- Determine when you want to achieve your goal. Be specific about the start date and the target completion date.

- Use phrases like "by the end of the year," "within three months," or "by July 15th" to make your timeframes clear and measurable.

BREAK DOWN YOUR GOAL:

- If your goal is substantial or long-term, break it down into smaller, more manageable milestones or phases.

- Assign deadlines to each milestone, allowing you to track progress and maintain motivation.

PRIORITIZE YOUR GOALS:

- If you have multiple goals, prioritize them based on their importance and urgency.

- Set deadlines accordingly, giving higher priority to goals that require immediate attention.

BE REALISTIC AND ACHIEVABLE:

- Ensure that the deadlines you set are realistic and attainable. Consider your resources, skills, and any potential obstacles.

- Avoid setting deadlines that are too tight, as this can lead to stress and reduced quality of work.

INCLUDE BUFFER TIME:

- Leave some buffer time in your timeline to account for unexpected delays, emergencies, or additional tasks that may arise.

- Buffer time can help you manage setbacks without derailing your overall progress.

CREATE A VISUAL TIMELINE:

- Visual representations, such as a calendar, Gantt chart, or project management software, can help you visualize yur timeline and deadlines.

- Seeing your goals and deadlines in a graphical format can make them feel more tangible and manageable.

REGULARLY REVIEW AND ADJUST:

- Periodically review your progress against the established timeline and deadlines.

- If you find that you are falling behind schedule or ahead of schedule, adjust your action plan and deadlines as needed.

STAY ACCOUNTABLE:

- Share your goals and associated deadlines with someone who can hold you accountable, such as a friend, mentor, or coach.

- Reporting your progress to someone else can help you stick to your timelines.

CELEBRATE MILESTONES:

- When you achieve milestones within your timeline, take the time to celebrate and acknowledge your progress.

- Celebrations can provide motivation and reinforce your commitment to the goal.

AVOID PROCRASTINATION:

- Deadlines can help combat procrastination by creating a sense of urgency. Use this motivation to tackle tasks promptly and efficiently.

STAY FLEXIBLE:

- While deadlines are essential, be willing to adjust them if necessary. Life may present unexpected challenges or opportunities, and flexibility is crucial.

USE POSITIVE REINFORCEMENT:

- Use positive self-talk and mental imagery to reinforce the importance of meeting your deadlines. Visualize the satisfaction and sense of achievement that comes with reaching your goals on time.

By incorporating timelines and deadlines into your goal-setting process, you create a structured and time-bound plan of action. This not only enhances your ability to track progress but also provides a framework for staying motivated and committed throughout your journey to achieving your goals

PRIOTIZATION

Evaluate the importance and urgency of the goal relative to your other objectives. Prioritize your goals to allocate your efforts wisely.

Prioritization is a critical aspect of goal setting that involves determining the relative importance and urgency of your goals and objectives. It helps you allocate your time, energy, and resources effectively to achieve the most meaningful and impactful outcomes. Here's how to prioritize your goals:

IDENTIFY YOUR GOALS:

- Start by listing all the goals you want to pursue in different areas of your life, such as career, personal development, health, and relationships.

CATEGORIZE YOUR GOALS:

- Group your goals into categories or areas of life, such as career, health and fitness, personal growth, family, and social.

CONSIDER YOUR VALUES AND LONG-TERM OBJECTIVES:

- Reflect on your values, aspirations, and long-term objectives. What matters most to you in the big picture of your life?

ASSESS IMPORTANCE AND IMPACT:

- Evaluate the importance and impact of each goal within its respective category. Consider how achieving each goal aligns with your values and contributes to your long-term vision.

USE A PRIORITY MATRIX:

- Create a priority matrix or table to help you visualize and compare the importance and urgency of each goal.

- Divide your goals into four quadrants:

- High Importance, High Urgency: These are your top priority goals that require immediate attention.

- High Importance, Low Urgency: These goals are important but may not need to be tackled right away. Schedule them for a specific timeframe.

- Low Importance, High Urgency: These goals may be urgent but less impactful. Consider delegating or minimizing time spent on them.

- Low Importance, Low Urgency: These goals are of low priority and can be considered for the future or deprioritized.

RANK WITHIN EACH CATEGORY:

- After categorizing and assessing the importance and urgency of your goals, rank them within each category. Identify the most critical goal in each category.

SET CLEAR PRIORITIES:

- Choose one or two top-priority goals in each category. These are the goals you will focus on and allocate the majority of your time and resources to.

CREATE AN ACTION PLAN:

- For your top-priority goals, create detailed action plans with specific steps and deadlines.

- Allocate resources, set milestones, and identify potential obstacles and solutions.

REVIEW AND REASSESS:

- Regularly review and reassess your priorities as circumstances change and you make progress on your goals.

- Adjust your priorities as needed to stay aligned with your values and long-term vision.

STAY FOCUSED:

- Concentrate your efforts on your top-priority goals to avoid spreading yourself too thin. Multitasking or pursuing too many goals simultaneously can dilute your effectiveness.

PRACTICE DISCIPLINE:

- Discipline yourself to stay on track with your prioritized goals, even when distractions or less important tasks arise

SEEK SUPPORT AND ACCOUNTABILITY:

- Share your priorities and goals with someone who can hold you accountable, provide guidance, and support your efforts.

- Maintain Balance:

- While focusing on top-priority goals, strive for balance in various areas of your life to ensure holistic well-being and fulfillment.

Prioritization in goal setting is about making intentional choices that align with your values and long-term vision. By concentrating your efforts on your most important and impactful goals, you can increase your effectiveness, achieve greater satisfaction, and make meaningful progress toward your desired outcomes.

OBSTACLES AND CHALLENGES

Anticipate potential obstacles and challenges that may arise during the pursuit of your goal. Identifying them in advance allows you to plan how to overcome them.

Obstacles and challenges are natural parts of the goal-setting process. While setting and pursuing goals is a valuable and rewarding endeavor, it often comes with its fair share of difficulties. Identifying potential obstacles and challenges in advance allows you to prepare for them and develop strategies to overcome them effectively. Here are some common obstacles and challenges you may encounter in goal setting:

LACK OF CLARITY:

- Unclear or vague goals can lead to confusion and indecision. When your goals are not well-defined, it's challenging to create a clear action plan.

PROCRASTINATION:

- Procrastination is a common challenge. It can prevent you from taking the necessary steps to achieve your goals.

LACK OF MOTIVATION:

- Sustaining motivation over the long term can be challenging. It's common to experience periods of low motivation, which can hinder progress.

TIME CONSTRAINTS:

- Balancing goal pursuit with daily responsibilities, such as work, family, and household chores, can be difficult.

FINANCIAL CONSTRAINTS:

- Some goals may require financial resources, and a lack of funds can be a significant obstacle.

FEAR OF FAILURE:

- The fear of failing to achieve a goal can be paralyzing. It may lead to self-doubt and a reluctance to take risks.

LACK OF SUPPORT:

- A lack of support from friends, family, or colleagues can make it harder to pursue and achieve your goals.

HEALTH ISSUES:

- Health problems or unexpected illnesses can disrupt your ability to work on your goals.

EXTERNAL EVENTS:

- External events, such as natural disasters, economic downturns, or unexpected life changes, can disrupt your plans.

OVERWHELM:

- Setting too many goals simultaneously or setting overly ambitious goals can lead to overwhelm and burnout.

LACK OF SKILLS OR KNOWLEDGE:

- Insufficient skills or knowledge in a particular area can be a significant obstacle when trying to achieve certain goals.

PERFECTIONISM:

- Striving for perfection can cause you to delay action or become overly critical of your progress.

DISTRACTIONS:

- Distractions from technology, social media, or other commitments can divert your attention away from your goals.

NEGATIVE SELF-TALK:

- Negative self-talk and self-limiting beliefs can undermine your confidence and motivation.

INERTIA AND COMFORT ZONE:

- It can be challenging to break out of your comfort zone and take the necessary steps to pursue ambitious goals.

LACK OF PLANNING:

- Insufficient planning, including a lack of clear action steps and timelines, can hinder goal progress.

UNFORESEEN OBSTACLES:

- There may be unexpected obstacles or challenges that arise during your journey that you couldn't have predicted.

To overcome these obstacles and challenges in goal setting:

- Set Clear Goals:

  Ensure your goals are specific, measurable, achievable, relevant, and time-bound (SMART) to enhance clarity.

- Develop Strategies:

  Create action plans that outline the specific steps you need to take to achieve your goals.

- Stay Motivated:

  Continuously remind yourself of your motivation and purpose behind your goals. Visualize the benefits of achieving them.

- Seek Support:

  Share your goals with supportive friends, family members, mentors, or coaches who can provide encouragement and guidance.

- Adapt and Adjust:

  Be flexible and willing to adapt your plans and strategies in response to unexpected challenges or changes in circumstances.

- Practice Self-Compassion:

  Be kind to yourself and acknowledge that setbacks and challenges are part of the journey. Learn from them and keep moving forward.

- Break Goals Into Smaller Steps:

  When faced with a significant challenge, break your goals down into smaller, more manageable steps to make progress more achievable.

- Celebrate Milestones:

  Celebrate your achievements along the way, even if they are small. This can help maintain motivation and a sense of accomplishment.

  Remember that encountering obstacles and challenges is a natural part of goal setting. How you respond to and overcome these challenges can ultimately determine your success in achieving your goals.

L e s s o n   9

MEASUREMENT AND TRACKING

Determine how you will measure your progress. What metrics or criteria will you use to assess your success?

Measurement and tracking are essential components of effective goal setting. They enable you to monitor your progress, make necessary adjustments, and stay motivated as you work toward your objectives. Here's how to incorporate measurement and tracking into your goal-setting process:

SET MEASURABLE GOALS:

- Ensure that your goals are specific and quantifiable. Use concrete metrics, such as numbers, percentages, or timeframes, to define success.

CHOOSE RELEVANT METRICS:

- Select metrics that are relevant to your goals and that accurately measure your progress and success.

- Consider using leading indicators (early warning signs) and lagging indicators (historical performance) to assess progress.

ESTABLISH BASELINE MEASUREMENTS:

- Before you start working on your goals, determine your starting point or baseline measurements. This provides a reference point for tracking progress.

CREATE A TRACKING SYSTEM:

- Develop a tracking system that allows you to record and monitor your progress regularly. This could be a spreadsheet, a journal, a goal-tracking app, or project management software.

SET MILESTONES AND CHECKPOINTS:

- Break your goals into smaller milestones or checkpoints that can be measured along the way.

- Assign specific metrics to each milestone to determine if you're on track

ASSIGN RESPONSIBILITY:

- Clearly define who is responsible for tracking progress. In some cases, this may be you, while in others, it could be a team member or a coach.

REGULARLY UPDATE YOUR TRACKING SYSTEM:

- Consistently record data and update your tracking system. The frequency of updates depends on the nature of your goals.

- Daily, weekly, or monthly updates are common, but choose a schedule that works for you.

VISUALIZE PROGRESS:

- Create visual representations of your progress, such as charts or graphs, to make it easier to see how you're doing.

REVIEW AND ANALYZE DATA:

- Periodically review and analyze the data you've collected. Look for trends, patterns, and areas where you may need to make adjustments.

CELEBRATE ACHIEVEMENTS:

- Celebrate your successes and achievements as you reach milestones or make progress toward your goal. This helps maintain motivation.

COURSE CORRECTION:

- If you notice that you're not making the expected progress, be prepared to make adjustments to your action plan or strategies.

STAY ACCOUNTABLE:

- Share your tracking and progress data with someone who can hold you accountable, such as a mentor, coach, or an accountability partner.

SEEK FEEDBACK:

- Don't hesitate to seek feedback from others who have experience with similar goals. They can provide valuable insights and guidance.

LEARN FROM SETBACKS:

- If you encounter setbacks or obstacles, use them as opportunities to learn and improve. Identify what went wrong and adjust your approach accordingly.

CONTINUOUS IMPROVEMENT:

- Continuously refine your tracking methods and the data you collect based on what you learn during your goal pursuit.

Measurement and tracking not only help you gauge your progress but also provide a sense of achievement and momentum. They ensure that you stay focused and committed to your goals and allow you to make data-driven decisions to improve your chances of success.

ACCOUNTABILITY

Share your goal with someone who can hold you accountable, such as a friend, family member, mentor, or coach.

Accountability is a powerful factor in goal setting and achievement. It involves taking responsibility for your actions and progress toward your goals and can significantly increase your likelihood of success. Here's how accountability works in the context of goal setting:

EXTERNAL ACCOUNTABILITY:

- External accountability involves involving someone else or a group of people in your goal-setting process to help keep you on track. These individuals can be friends, family members, mentors, coaches, or colleagues.

INTERNAL ACCOUNTABILITY:

- Internal accountability is the personal commitment and responsibility you have to yourself to achieve your goals. It's about being self-disciplined and holding yourself to a high standard.

BENEFITS OF ACCOUNTABILITY:

- Motivation: Knowing that you are accountable to someone else can provide an extra level of motivation to work toward your goals consistently.

- Commitment: Accountability reinforces your commitment to your goals, making it less likely that you'll give up when faced with challenges.

- Feedback: Accountability partners can provide valuable feedback, guidance, and insights based on their experiences and perspectives.

- Progress Tracking: Accountability helps you track your progress and stay on schedule, increasing the likelihood of meeting your deadlines.

- Increased Likelihood of Success: Studies have shown that individuals who have accountability partners are more likely to achieve their goals.

WAYS TO INCORPORATE ACCOUNTABILITY IN GOAL SETTING:

- Share Your Goals: Inform someone you trust about your goals and discuss your action plan with them. This creates a sense of commitment.

- Set Up Regular Check-Ins: Schedule regular meetings or check-ins with your accountability partner to review your progress and discuss any challenges or adjustments needed.

- Use Accountability Tools: Utilize technology or apps designed for tracking and sharing progress. Some goal-tracking apps allow you to share your progress with a network of friends or peers.

- Join a Support Group: Participate in a support group or community of individuals who share similar goals. These groups can offer encouragement, motivation, and a sense of camaraderie.

- Hire a Coach or Mentor: Consider working with a coach or mentor who specializes in the area related to your goals. They can provide personalized guidance and accountability.

- Create a Public Commitment: Share your goals on social media or with a larger audience if you're comfortable doing so. The public commitment can provide additional motivation.

ACCOUNTABILITY GUIDELINES:

- Choose the Right Partner: Select an accountability partner or group that is supportive, trustworthy, and genuinely interested in your success.

- Be Specific: Clearly define your expectations and responsibilities with your accountability partner. Discuss how often you'll check in and what kind of feedback or support you need.

- Be Honest: Be open and honest about your progress and challenges. Accountability works best when you're transparent about both successes and setbacks.

- Use Positive Reinforcement: Encourage and celebrate each other's achievements. Positive reinforcement can boost motivation and morale.

- Stay Committed: Both you and your accountability partner should stay committed to the process. If one party is not fully engaged, the effectiveness of accountability may diminish.

Remember that accountability is not about placing blame or judgment but about providing support and encouragement to help you stay focused and make progress toward your goals. Whether it's external or internal accountability, it can be a valuable tool in your goal-setting toolkit.

REVIEW AND EVALUATION

Regularly review your progress toward the goal. Assess what's working and what isn't. Adjust your action plan as needed.

Review and evaluation are essential steps in the goal-setting process as they allow you to assess your progress, identify areas for improvement, and make informed decisions about your goals. Regularly reviewing and evaluating your goals can help you stay on track and increase your chances of success. Here's how to incorporate review and evaluation into your goal-setting process:

SET REVIEW MILESTONES:

- Determine specific points in time when you will review your progress. These milestones can be daily, weekly, monthly, or at key stages in your goal pursuit.

USE MEASURABLE METRICS:

- Ensure that your goals are measurable and quantifiable from the start. This makes it easier to track your progress and measure success objectively.

COLLECT DATA:

- Gather data and information related to your goals. This could include numbers, performance metrics, feedback, observations, and any relevant documentation.

ASSESS PROGRESS:

- Analyze the data you've collected to assess your progress. Compare your current status to your baseline measurements or desired outcomes.

CELEBRATE ACHIEVEMENTS:

- Acknowledge and celebrate your achievements, no matter how small they may seem. Celebrating progress can boost motivation and morale.

IDENTIFY CHALLENGES AND OBSTACLES:

- Identify any challenges, obstacles, or setbacks you've encountered during your pursuit of the goal. Understanding what went wrong can help you make improvements.

ADJUST STRATEGIES:

- If you find that your current strategies are not yielding the desired results, be open to adjusting your action plan. Adapt your approach based on your evaluation findings.

SEEK FEEDBACK:

- If applicable, seek feedback from mentors, coaches, or trusted individuals who can provide valuable insights and suggestions for improvement.

REFLECT ON YOUR EFFORTS:

- Reflect on your personal commitment and effort toward the goal. Are you consistently working toward it? Are there areas where you could improve your dedication?

CONSIDER ENVIRONMENTAL FACTORS:

- Assess how external factors, such as changes in the market, economic conditions, or personal circumstances, have influenced your progress.

REEVALUATE GOAL RELEVANCE:

- Ensure that your goals remain relevant to your life and aspirations. As circumstances change, your goals may need to be adjusted or replaced with new ones.

STAY ADAPTABLE:

- Be flexible and willing to adapt your goals, strategies, and timelines based on your review and evaluation findings.

LEARN FROM SETBACKS:

- Use setbacks as learning opportunities. Analyze what caused the setback and how you can prevent or address similar challenges in the future.

MAINTAIN A GROWTH MINDSET:

- Embrace a growth mindset, which means viewing challenges and failures as opportunities for growth and learning rather than as roadblocks.

RECORD YOUR FINDINGS:

- Keep a record of your review and evaluation findings. Document what you've learned and the adjustments you've made.

SET NEW GOALS:

- Based on your evaluations, set new goals or refine existing ones to reflect your evolving priorities and aspirations.

CONTINUOUSLY IMPROVE:

- Use the insights gained from your evaluations to continuously improve your goal-setting and goal-achieving strategies.

Regularly reviewing and evaluating your goals is a dynamic process that ensures you stay aligned with your objectives and make necessary adjustments along the way. It helps you maintain focus, learn from your experiences, and increase your chances of achieving your desired outcomes.

L e s s o n   1 2

REWARDS AND CELEBRATIONS

Define how you will celebrate your achievements and milestones along the way. Rewarding yourself can reinforce motivation.

Rewards and celebrations play a crucial role in the goal-setting process. They serve as incentives, motivation, and acknowledgments of your achievements along the journey to your goals. Incorporating rewards and celebrations can make the pursuit of your goals more enjoyable and satisfying. Here's how to use rewards and celebrations effectively in goal setting:

1. DEFINE REWARD MILESTONES:

Break your larger goal into smaller milestones or checkpoints. For each milestone, set a specific reward that you'll give yourself upon successful completion.

- These rewards can act as positive reinforcement for your progress.

2. CHOOSE MEANINGFUL REWARDS:

- Select rewards that are personally meaningful and aligned with your interests and values. The more meaningful the reward, the more motivating it will be.

- Rewards can vary widely, from simple treats like a favorite snack to larger rewards like a weekend getaway.

3. MAKE THEM PROPORTIONAL:

- Match the size of the reward to the significance of the milestone. Smaller milestones may warrant smaller rewards, while larger achievements deserve more substantial rewards.

4. CELEBRATE ACHIEVEMENTS:

- Celebrate your achievements when you reach milestones or successfully complete your goals. Celebrations can include sharing the accomplishment with loved ones, going out for a special meal, or taking a day off to relax.

5. TRACK PROGRESS TOWARD REWARDS:

- Keep track of your progress toward earning rewards. This can help you stay motivated and focused on the goal.

- Use a checklist or a visual chart to mark off completed milestones.

6. SET NON-FOOD REWARDS:

- While it's common to use food or indulgences as rewards, consider incorporating non-food rewards to avoid unhealthy habits. Non-food rewards could include a spa day, a new book, or a hobby-related purchase.

7. CELEBRATE PERSONAL GROWTH:

- Celebrate not only the achievement of the goal itself but also the personal growth, skills, and lessons you've gained along the way. Recognize and appreciate your journey.

8. SHARE YOUR SUCCESS:

- Share your success with friends and family. They can provide additional support and celebrate with you.

9. PLAN AHEAD:

- Plan your rewards and celebrations in advance, so they are ready to go when you reach your milestones or accomplish your goals. This can make the process more motivating.

10. BE MINDFUL OF FREQUENCY:

- Be cautious about overindulging or rewarding yourself too frequently, as it can diminish the impact of rewards. Reserve rewards for significant achievements.

11. INCORPORATE INTRINSIC REWARDS:

- In addition to external rewards, find intrinsic rewards in your goal pursuit. Enjoy the satisfaction of progress, personal growth, and the journey itself.

12. SET NEW GOALS:

- After achieving a goal and celebrating your success, consider setting new goals to maintain motivation and continue your personal development.

13. MAINTAIN BALANCE:

- While rewards and celebrations are important, maintain a balance between treating yourself and staying disciplined in your goal pursuit.

14. REFLECT ON ACHIEVEMENTS:

- Take time to reflect on your achievements during celebrations. Express gratitude for the effort you've put in and the results you've achieved.

Remember that rewards and celebrations are not just about external recognition; they also serve to reinforce your commitment, boost motivation, and create positive associations with your goals. By incorporating rewards and celebrations into your goal-setting process, you can make the journey more enjoyable and increase your chances of success.

FLEXIBILITY AND ADAPTABILITY

Be open to adapting your goals or strategies if circumstances change. Being flexible can help you stay on track.

Flexibility and adaptability are essential qualities to have when pursuing goals. The ability to adjust your plans and strategies as circumstances change can greatly enhance your chances of success. Here's how flexibility and adaptability fit into the goal-setting process:

RECOGNIZE THE DYNAMIC NATURE OF LIFE:

- Understand that life is inherently unpredictable. External factors, unexpected events, and changing priorities can all impact your ability to pursue and achieve your goals.

SET REALISTIC EXPECTATIONS:

- While it's important to set ambitious goals, also be realistic about potential challenges and obstacles that may arise along the way.

EMBRACE A GROWTH MINDSET:

- Cultivate a growth mindset, which means viewing challenges and setbacks as opportunities for learning and growth rather than as failures. This mindset fosters resilience and adaptability.

REGULARLY REVIEW PROGRESS:

- Periodically assess your progress and the effectiveness of your strategies. Ask yourself if your current approach is yielding the expected results.

IDENTIFY CHANGING PRIORITIES:

- As circumstances change, your priorities may shift. It's okay to reevaluate your goals and make adjustments to ensure they align with your evolving interests and values.

BE OPEN TO FEEDBACK:

- Seek feedback from mentors, coaches, or trusted individuals who can provide insights and suggestions for improvement. Be receptive to constructive criticism.

MODIFY ACTION PLANS:

- When faced with challenges or when your current strategies are not working, be willing to modify your action plan. Adapt your approach to address new information or obstacles.

SHIFT TIMELINES WHEN NECESSARY:

- Adjust your timelines or deadlines if you encounter delays or unexpected setbacks. It's better to extend your timeframe and succeed than to rush and compromise quality.

PIVOT WHEN APPROPRIATE:

- Sometimes, a significant change in direction, or a pivot, may be necessary. Be open to making major adjustments to your goals if your original plan is no longer feasible or relevant.

SEEK NEW OPPORTUNITIES:

- Stay open to new opportunities that may arise during your goal pursuit. Sometimes, an unexpected opportunity can lead to greater success than your initial plan.

BALANCE PERSEVERANCE AND ADAPTATION:

- While it's important to persevere and stay committed to your goals, also recognize when it's time to adapt. Balancing these qualities is key to success.

MAINTAIN CORE VALUES:

- While adapting to changing circumstances, ensure that your core values and principles remain intact. Don't compromise your values in the pursuit of a goal.

LEARN FROM SETBACKS:

- When faced with setbacks or failures, analyze what went wrong and apply the lessons learned to improve your future efforts.

STAY AGILE:

- Approach your goals with agility, meaning the ability to make quick, effective, and well-informed decisions in response to changing conditions.

STAY RESILIENT:

- Resilience is the ability to bounce back from setbacks. Develop resilience by building your emotional and mental strength to navigate challenges.

PLAN FOR CONTINGENCIES:

- Anticipate potential obstacles and have contingency plans in place. Knowing how to respond to challenges can help you adapt more effectively.

STAY FOCUSED ON THE OUTCOME:

- While adapting to changing circumstances, keep your ultimate goal in mind. Adaptation is a means to achieving your end objective, not a deviation from it.

Flexibility and adaptability are not signs of weakness but rather strengths that enable you to navigate the complex and unpredictable journey of goal setting. Embracing these qualities can help you stay resilient, maintain your momentum, and ultimately achieve your desired outcomes.

DOCUMENTATION

Write down your goal and the accompanying action plan. Documenting your goals makes them tangible and reinforces your commitment.

Documentation is a crucial aspect of goal setting and achievement. Keeping clear and organized records of your goals, plans, progress, and outcomes can help you stay focused, accountable, and effective throughout the process. Here's how documentation plays a vital role in goal setting:

GOAL CLARITY:

- Documenting your goals in writing helps clarify and solidify your intentions. When you articulate your goals clearly, you have a better understanding of what you want to achieve.

ACTION PLANS:

- Create detailed action plans that outline the specific steps, tasks, and timelines required to reach your goals. Documenting your action plan makes it easier to follow and monitor progress.

ACCOUNTABILITY:

- Documenting your goals and sharing them with others, such as accountability partners or mentors, creates a sense of responsibility and helps you stay on track.

PROGRESS TRACKING:

- Keep a record of your progress by regularly documenting the steps you've completed, milestones achieved, and relevant metrics or data. This tracking allows you to measure your success objectively.

DATA AND METRICS:

- Collect and document data and metrics related to your goals. This could include financial records, performance indicators, or any quantifiable information that reflects your progress.

REFLECTION AND LEARNING:

- Maintain a journal or diary where you reflect on your experiences, setbacks, and successes. Documenting your reflections can provide valuable insights for future goal-setting endeavors.

VISUAL AIDS:

- Use visual aids such as charts, graphs, or progress trackers to represent your goals and monitor your progress. Visual documentation can make it easier to see trends and patterns.

REVIEW AND EVALUATION:

- Document the results of your reviews and evaluations, including what worked well and what didn't. This documentation helps you make informed decisions about your goals

ADJUSTMENTS AN ADAPTATIONS:

- If you need to make adjustments or adapt your strategies, document these changes and the reasons behind them. This ensures you have a clear record of your decision-making process.

COMMUNICATION:

- Use written communication to share updates, progress reports, and goal-related information with others who are involved or interested in your goals.

LEGAL AND COMPLIANCE:

- In some cases, particularly for business or financial goals, documentation is essential for legal and compliance purposes. Keep records that adhere to legal requirements.

ACCOUNTABILITY PARTNERS:

- If you have accountability partners or mentors, share your documentation with them to keep them informed and engaged in your goal pursuit.

CELEBRATION AND REWARDS:

- Document your celebrations and rewards as you achieve milestones or successfully complete goals. This can serve as a record of your accomplishments and motivation.

TRANSPARENCY:

- Transparent documentation of your goals and progress can foster trust and credibility with stakeholders, whether they are personal or professional.

HISTORICAL PERSPECTIVE:

- Over time, your documentation becomes a valuable historical record of your goals and achievements. It can be a source of motivation and inspiration for future endeavors.

GOAL SETTING ITERATION:

- Reviewing past documentation can help you refine your goal-setting process and learn from previous experiences, leading to more effective future goals.

Choose the documentation methods and tools that work best for you. This could include digital tools like spreadsheets, project management software, or physical journals and notebooks. The key is to establish a system that allows you to capture and organize the information relevant to your goals effectively. Effective documentation not only helps you achieve your current goals but also serves as a valuable resource for your ongoing personal and professional development.

REFLECTION AND LEARNING

Reflect on your experiences and what you've learned throughout the goal-setting process. Apply these insights to future goals.

Reflection and learning are integral components of the goal-setting process. They allow you to gain insights from your experiences, adapt your strategies, and continuously improve as you work toward your objectives. Here's how reflection and learning fit into goal setting:

REGULAR SELF-ASSESSMENT:

- Set aside dedicated time for self-assessment and reflection. This could be daily, weekly, or monthly, depending on the nature and timeline of your goals.

JOURNALING:

- Maintain a journal or diary where you document your thoughts, feelings, challenges, and successes related to your goals. This written record can help you process your experiences.

REVIEW PROGRESS:

- Periodically review your progress toward your goals. Consider what you've accomplished, what's still ahead, and any adjustments you've made to your action plan.

IDENTIFY LESSONS LEARNED:

- Reflect on the lessons you've learned from your experiences. What worked well? What didn't? What would you do differently next time?

ANALYZE SETBACKS AND CHALLENGES:

- Pay close attention to setbacks and challenges you've encountered. Analyze the root causes and determine how to address or avoid similar issues in the future.

ACKNOWLEDGE ACHIEVEMENTS:

- Celebrate your achievements, no matter how small they may seem. Reflect on the effort you put in and the progress you've made.

EMBRACE A GROWTH MINDSET:

- Cultivate a growth mindset, which means viewing failures or setbacks as opportunities for growth and learning rather than as indicators of inadequacy.

SEEK FEEDBACK:

- Seek feedback from mentors, coaches, or trusted individuals who can provide constructive insights and suggestions for improvement.

VISUALIZE SUCCESS:

- Use visualization techniques to imagine yourself achieving your goals. Visualization can help boost confidence and motivation.

ADJUST STRATEGIES:

- Based on your reflections and what you've learned, be willing to adjust your strategies and action plans as needed.

STAY OPEN-MINDED:

- Be open to new ideas, approaches, and solutions that may arise during your reflection process. Sometimes, fresh perspectives can lead to breakthroughs.

SET NEW GOALS:

- After achieving a goal, consider setting new ones that build upon what you've learned and accomplished. Continuous goal setting keeps you motivated and growing.

STAY COMMITTED TO SELF-IMPROVEMENT:

- Make self-improvement and personal growth a priority in your goal-setting journey. Commit to becoming the best version of yourself.

SHARE YOUR INSIGHTS:

- Share your insights and reflections with others who may benefit from your experiences. Teaching what you've learned can deepen your understanding and reinforce your knowledge.

REVIEW PAST DOCUMENTATION:

- Refer to past documentation, such as journals or progress reports, to review your journey. This historical perspective can be a valuable source of inspiration and guidance.

PRACTICE SELF-COMPASSION:

- Be kind and compassionate toward yourself during the reflection process. Avoid harsh self-criticism and focus on constructive self-feedback.

STAY PATIENT AND PERSISTENT:

- Understand that reflection and learning are ongoing processes. Goals may take time to achieve, and you may need to adapt continuously.

Reflection and learning help you make informed decisions, refine your strategies, and maintain motivation throughout your goal-setting journey. By integrating these practices into your routine, you can enhance your ability to achieve your goals and develop as an individual or professional.

COMMUNICATION

If your goal involves others, communicate your objectives clearly and involve them in the planning and execution as necessary.

Effective communication is essential in goal setting, as it plays a vital role in articulating your goals, gaining support, and maintaining alignment among individuals or teams working toward a common objective. Here's how communication functions within the goal-setting process:

CLARITY OF GOALS:

- Clearly communicate your goals in a concise and understandable manner. Use specific, measurable, achievable, relevant, and time-bound (SMART) language to articulate what you want to achieve.

SHARE YOUR VISION:

- Explain the broader vision or purpose behind your goals. Help others understand why these goals are important and how they fit into the bigger picture

STAKEHOLDER INVOLVEMENT:

- Involve relevant stakeholders, such as team members, colleagues, or family members, in the goal-setting process. Solicit their input and feedback to create a shared sense of ownership.

SET EXPECTATIONS:

- Clearly define roles, responsibilities, and expectations for all parties involved. Make sure everyone understands their contributions and commitments.

REGULAR UPDATES:

- Maintain open and consistent communication channels to provide regular updates on progress, challenges, and successes related to your goals.

FEEDBACK LOOP:

- Encourage feedback from team members or accountability partners. Create a feedback loop where everyone feels comfortable sharing insights and suggestions.

PROBLEM SOLVING:

- Communicate openly when obstacles or challenges arise. Collaborate with others to identify solutions and overcome setbacks.

CELEBRATE ACHIEVEMENTS:

- Celebrate milestones and successes as a team or with individuals who support your goals. Recognition and celebration help maintain motivation and morale.

TRANSPARENT REPORTING:

- Ensure transparency in reporting progress and outcomes. Honest and accurate reporting builds trust and credibility.

ADJUSTMENTS AND ADAPTATIONS:

- Communicate any necessary adjustments to your goals or action plans as circumstances change. Explain the reasons for changes and the expected impact.

CLARIFY DEADLINES:

- Clearly communicate deadlines and timeframes associated with your goals. Ensure everyone understands the sense of urgency and the importance of meeting deadlines.

CONFLICT RESOLUTION:

- Address conflicts or disagreements among team members promptly and constructively. Effective communication is essential for resolving conflicts and maintaining team cohesion.

ALIGN PERSONAL AND ORGANIZATIONAL GOALS:

- In a professional setting, ensure that individual and team goals align with the broader organizational goals. Effective communication helps create synergy among different levels of objectives.

FEEDBACK AND EVALUATION:

- Request and provide feedback during the evaluation of goal progress. This feedback can inform improvements in strategies and performance

DOCUMENT AGREEMENTS:

- Document important agreements, decisions, and action plans resulting from discussions. Written documentation helps prevent misunderstandings and provides a reference point.

USE MULTIPLE COMMUNICATION CHANNELS:

- Employ various communication channels, such as meetings, emails, messaging apps, and project management tools, to ensure that information flows efficiently.

ADAPT COMMUNICATION STYLES:

- Recognize that different individuals have different communication styles and preferences. Adapt your approach to ensure effective communication with diverse stakeholders.

LISTENING SKILLS:

- Cultivate active listening skills to fully understand the perspectives and concerns of others. Listening promotes empathy and strengthens relationships.

Effective communication is a two-way process that involves both conveying your message clearly and actively listening to others. By fostering open and transparent communication, you can build stronger relationships, create a supportive environment for goal achievement, and ensure that everyone involved remains informed, engaged, and motivated throughout the goal-setting journey.

CONTINUOUS IMPROVEMENT

Use the knowledge and skills you gain while pursuing your goal to improve yourself and your approach to future goals.

Continuous improvement is a fundamental principle in goal setting that involves refining your goal-setting process over time to enhance its effectiveness. It's about learning from your experiences, making adjustments, and applying insights to set and achieve future goals more efficiently. Here are key steps to implement continuous improvement in goal setting:

REFLECT ON PAST GOALS:

- Begin by reflecting on your past goal-setting experiences. What worked well? What could have been done better? Analyze your successes and any areas where you fell short.

SET IMPROVEMENT GOALS:

- Set specific improvement goals for your goal-setting process. For example, you might aim to set more focused goals, improve your tracking methods, or enhance your time management skills.

REVIEW GOAL-SETTING METHODS:

- Evaluate your current goal-setting methods, including how you define goals, create action plans, and track progress. Identify any areas that could be refined or streamlined.

LEARN FROM SETBACKS:

- Embrace setbacks as opportunities for learning and growth. Analyze what went wrong and why. Use this information to avoid similar issues in the future.

EMBRACE FEEDBACK:

- Seek feedback from mentors, accountability partners, or colleagues who have experience with goal setting. They can offer valuable insights and suggestions for improvement.

STUDY BEST PRACTICES:

- Stay informed about best practices in goal setting and achievement. Books, articles, workshops, and courses can provide valuable knowledge and strategies.

EXPERIMENT WITH NEW APPROACHES:

- Be open to trying new goal-setting approaches or techniques. Experiment with different methods to see what works best for you.

REFINE YOUR ACTION PLANS:

- Continuously refine your action plans. Break down your goals into smaller, manageable steps, and be as specific as possible about the actions required.

REGULARLY EVALUATE PROGRESS:

- Implement a system for regularly evaluating your progress. This can include tracking metrics, milestones, and checkpoints to ensure you stay on course.

ADAPT TO CHANGING CIRCUMSTANCES:

- Recognize that circumstances can change, and your goals may need to evolve accordingly. Be adaptable and willing to adjust your goals when necessary.

BALANCE AMBITION AND REALISM:

- Strive for ambitious goals but also ensure they are realistic and achievable. Avoid setting goals that are too overwhelming or out of reach.

MAINTAIN FOCUS ON KEY PRIORITIES:

- Continuously assess your priorities and ensure that your goals align with them. Avoid spreading yourself too thin with too many objectives.

TRACK YOUR GROWTH:

- Document your personal growth and development as a result of your goal-setting efforts. Recognize how you've improved as a goal-setter and goal-achiever.

CELEBRATE IMPROVEMENT:

- Celebrate your progress in refining your goal-setting process. Acknowledge your efforts to become a more effective goal setter.

SET NEW GOALS:

- Apply what you've learned from your continuous improvement efforts to set new, more impactful goals. Use your insights to set objectives that are even better aligned with your aspirations.

SHARE INSIGHTS:

- Share your insights and experiences with others who may benefit from your knowledge. Teaching what you've learned can reinforce your own understanding.

STAY PATIENT AND PERSISTENT:

- Continuous improvement takes time. Be patient with yourself as you refine your goal-setting skills, and remain persistent in your pursuit of excellence.

By embracing continuous improvement in goal setting, you can enhance your ability to set meaningful goals, achieve them more efficiently, and experience personal and professional growth. The goal-setting process should evolve and adapt to your changing needs and experiences, ultimately helping you realize your aspirations more effectively.

By addressing these key components, you can create a comprehensive goal-setting framework that increases your chances of success and provides a roadmap for achieving your personal and professional objectives.

ELEMENTS OF EFFECTIVE GOAL SETTING

SPECIFIC:

Goals should be clear and well-defined. Vague goals are less likely to be achieved because they lack focus.

- Goals should be clearly defined and specific. Avoid vague or broad objectives.

- Ask yourself: What exactly do I want to achieve? Be precise in your description.

MEASURABLE:

Goals should be quantifiable, allowing you to track progress and determine when they have been achieved.

- Goals should be quantifiable so that you can track your progress objectively.

- Ask yourself: How will I measure or determine when the goal has been achieved? What metrics or criteria will I use?

ACHIEVABLE:

Your goals should be realistic and attainable. Setting goals that are too far out of reach can lead to frustration and demotivation.

- Goals should be realistic and attainable, given your resources, skills, and constraints.

- Ask yourself: Is this goal within my reach, or is it too challenging? Can I realistically accomplish it?

RELEVANT:

Goals should align with your values, long-term objectives, and overall mission. They should be meaningful to you.

- Goals should be relevant and aligned with your values, long-term objectives, and overall mission.

- Ask yourself: Is this goal meaningful and worthwhile in the context of my life or work?

TIME-BOUND:

Goals should have a specific timeframe or deadline for completion. This creates a sense of urgency and helps you prioritize your efforts.

- Goals should have a specific timeframe or deadline for completion. This creates a sense of urgency and helps you prioritize your efforts.

- Ask yourself: By when do I want to achieve this goal? What's the deadline?

Effective goal setting involves several key elements that help you define, plan, and achieve your objectives in a focused and systematic manner. These elements are often encapsulated in the SMART criteria, which stands for Specific, Measurable, Achievable, Relevant, and Time-bound. Here's a breakdown of each element:

ADDITION:

In addition to the SMART criteria, there are other key elements to consider when setting effective goals:

Clear and Concise Language:

- Use clear and straightforward language when defining your goals. Avoid jargon or overly complex terms.

- Make sure anyone reading your goals can easily understand what you're trying to achieve.

Positive and Inspirational:

- Frame your goals in a positive and inspiring manner. Focus on what you want to achieve rather than what you want to avoid.

- Use language that motivates and excites you, reinforcing your commitment to the goal.

Written and Documented:

- Write down your goals. Putting them on paper (or in a digital format) makes them tangible and reinforces your commitment.

- Documenting your goals allows you to review and track your progress over time.

Challenging but Realistic:

- While goals should be challenging enough to push you out of your comfort zone, they should also be realistic. Ensure that they are achievable with the resources and skills at your disposal.

Breakdown into Action Steps:

- Divide larger goals into smaller, manageable steps or milestones. This makes the process less overwhelming and helps you plan your actions.

Prioritization:

- Evaluate the importance and urgency of each goal. Focus on the goals that align most closely with your current priorities.

Flexibility and Adaptability:

- Be willing to adapt your goals or strategies if circumstances change. Sometimes, adjustments are necessary to stay on track.

Regular Review:

- Continuously review your goals to ensure they remain relevant and align with your evolving aspirations and circumstances.

By incorporating these key elements into your goal-setting process, you can increase your chances of success and create a roadmap for achieving your personal and professional objectives effectively.

PART 3

BENEFITS OF GOAL SETTING

Lesson 19

CLARITY

Goals provide a sense of direction, helping you understand what you want to achieve and why it matters.

Clarity is a foundational principle in goal setting. When your goals are clear, they are easier to understand, focus on, and achieve. Here's why clarity is essential and how to ensure clarity in your goal-setting process:

IMPORTANCE OF CLARITY IN GOAL SETTING:

Clear Direction:

Clarity provides a clear sense of direction and purpose. When your goals are crystal clear, you know exactly what you are working toward.

Motivation:

Clear goals are more motivating. They give you a compelling reason to take action and stay committed, as you can see the desired outcome clearly.

Focus:

Clarity helps you stay focused on what matters most. It reduces distractions and prevents you from getting sidetracked by less important tasks.

Effective Planning:

When your goals are clear, you can create precise action plans that outline the steps required to achieve them.

Measurement:

Clear goals are measurable. You can easily track your progress and determine whether you are moving closer to your desired outcome.

HOW TO ENSURE CLARITY IN GOAL SETTING:

USE THE SMART CRITERIA:

- Apply the SMART criteria to your goals:
  - ☐ Specific: Clearly define what you want to achieve.
  - ☐ Measurable: Identify specific metrics or indicators of success.
  - ☐ Achievable: Ensure your goals are realistic and attainable.
  - ☐ Relevant: Make sure your goals align with your values and priorities.
  - ☐ Time-bound: Set a deadline or timeframe for achieving your goals.

Be Specific:

- Avoid vague or general goals. Instead of saying "I want to get fit," specify "I want to lose 20 pounds in six months by following a healthy diet and exercising three times a week."

Break Goals into Smaller Steps:

- Divide larger goals into smaller, actionable steps. This makes the path to achieving your goals more manageable and clear.

Visualize Your Goals:

- Create a clear mental image of what success looks like. Visualization can help you see and feel the outcome, enhancing clarity and motivation.

Write Your Goals Down:

- Document your goals in writing. This not only clarifies your objectives but also creates a tangible commitment.

Use Clear Language:

- Use plain and straightforward language to describe your goals. Avoid jargon or overly technical terms.

Avoid Ambiguity:

- Eliminate any ambiguity from your goals. Each goal should have a single, well-defined interpretation.

Get Feedback:

- Share your goals with a trusted friend, mentor, or coach to ensure they understand your objectives. Their feedback can help refine your goals.

Review and Revise:

- Regularly review your goals to ensure they remain clear and relevant. Revise them as needed to reflect changes in your circumstances or priorities.

Prioritize Goals:

- Clarify your most important goals. Prioritization helps you focus your time and energy on what truly matters.

Align with Values:

- Ensure your goals align with your personal values and long-term aspirations. Goals that resonate with your values are more likely to be clear and motivating.

Keep It Simple:

- Simplicity aids clarity. Avoid overly complex or convoluted goals that may be difficult to understand or achieve.

Create a Vision Board:

- Consider creating a vision board that visually represents your goals. This can serve as a constant reminder and reinforce clarity.

Regularly Communicate:

- Keep the lines of communication open with others involved in your goals, whether they are personal or professional. Ensure everyone has a clear understanding of objectives.

By prioritizing clarity in your goal-setting process, you can increase your chances of success, maintain motivation, and make more efficient progress toward your desired outcomes. Clear goals serve as a guiding light, helping you navigate the path to your aspirations with confidence and purpose.

MOTIVATION

Having clear goals can boost your motivation and drive, making it easier to stay focused and work diligently.

Motivation plays a crucial role in goal setting, as it provides the drive and energy needed to pursue and achieve your objectives. Here are strategies for harnessing motivation in the goal-setting process:

1. DEFINE YOUR "WHY":

- Understand the deeper reasons behind your goals. Ask yourself why each goal is important to you and how achieving it aligns with your values and aspirations. A strong "why" can fuel your motivation.

2. SET MEANINGFUL GOALS:

- Choose goals that have personal significance to you. Goals that resonate with your passions and values are more likely to motivate you.

3. MAKE YOUR GOALS SMART:

- Use the SMART criteria (Specific, Measurable, Achievable, Relevant, Time-bound) to make your goals clear and tangible. This clarity can boost motivation by providing a clear target.

4. BREAK GOALS INTO SMALLER STEPS:

- Divide larger goals into smaller, manageable steps. Achieving these mini-milestones can provide a sense of accomplishment and maintain motivation.

5. VISUALIZE SUCCESS:

- Create a vivid mental picture of yourself achieving your goals. Visualizing success can make your objectives feel more attainable and keep you motivated.

6. CREATE A VISION BOARD:

- Compile images, quotes, and visual representations of your goals on a vision board. Display it prominently to serve as a daily reminder of your aspirations.

7. DEVELOP A PLAN:

- Create a well-defined action plan that outlines the steps required to achieve your goals. A clear roadmap helps maintain focus and motivation.

8. SET DEADLINES:

- Establish specific deadlines for your goals. Time-bound objectives create a sense of urgency and prevent procrastination.

9. FIND ACCOUNTABILITY PARTNERS:

- Share your goals with trusted friends, mentors, or accountability partners who can provide support, encouragement, and accountability.

10. CELEBRATE MILESTONES:

- Acknowledge and celebrate your achievements, even small ones. Celebrations can boost motivation and reinforce positive behaviors.

11. STAY INSPIRED:

- Surround yourself with sources of inspiration. Read books, listen to podcasts, or engage with individuals who have achieved similar goals.

12. STAY POSITIVE:

- Maintain a positive mindset. Focus on your strengths and past successes to build confidence in your ability to achieve your goals.

13. OVERCOME OBSTACLES:

- Identify potential obstacles and develop strategies for overcoming them. A problem-solving mindset can help you stay motivated in the face of challenges.

14. STAY FLEXIBLE:

- Be open to adjusting your goals and strategies as needed. Flexibility can help you navigate unexpected setbacks without losing motivation.

15. TRACK PROGRESS:

- Keep a record of your progress. Regularly reviewing your achievements can provide a sense of accomplishment and motivation to keep going.

16. VISUAL AND VERBAL AFFIRMATIONS:

- Use positive affirmations or mantras to reinforce your belief in your ability to achieve your goals. Repeating these affirmations can boost confidence.

17. FIND INTRINSIC MOTIVATION:

- Seek internal sources of motivation, such as personal fulfillment, growth, and a sense of purpose. Intrinsic motivation tends to be more sustainable than extrinsic rewards.

18. STAY PERSISTENT:

- Understand that motivation can fluctuate. During periods of low motivation, rely on discipline and commitment to keep moving forward.

19. REVIEW YOUR "WHY" REGULARLY:

- Periodically revisit your reasons for pursuing your goals. Remind yourself of the meaningful "why" behind each objective.

20. LEARN FROM SETBACKS:

- Instead of being discouraged by setbacks, view them as learning opportunities. Analyze what went wrong and use the lessons to adjust your approach.

Motivation is not constant, but by incorporating these strategies into your goal-setting process, you can maintain and even boost your motivation over time. Remember that motivation often grows stronger as you make progress and see results, so taking consistent action toward your goals is a key factor in staying motivated.

FOCUS

Goals help you concentrate your efforts on tasks and activities that move you closer to your desired outcomes.

Maintaining focus is essential in goal setting because it helps you stay on track, avoid distractions, and channel your energy and resources toward achieving your objectives. Here are strategies to enhance your focus in the goal-setting process:

1. PRIORITIZE YOUR GOALS:

- Identify your most important goals and prioritize them. Focusing on a limited number of objectives at a time increases your chances of success.

2. SET CLEAR AND SPECIFIC GOALS:

- Use the SMART criteria to make your goals clear, specific, and well-defined. A precise goal provides a clear target for your focus.

3. BREAK GOALS INTO SMALLER STEPS:

- Divide larger goals into smaller, manageable tasks or milestones. This makes it easier to maintain focus on individual actions.

4. CREATE A DETAILED ACTION PLAN:

- Develop a comprehensive action plan that outlines the steps required to achieve your goals. Having a roadmap enhances your focus on what needs to be done.

5. ELIMINATE DISTRACTIONS:

- Identify common distractions in your environment and work to minimize or eliminate them. This might include turning off notifications, setting specific work hours, or creating a dedicated workspace.

6. TIME MANAGEMENT:

- Use effective time management techniques, such as the Pomodoro Technique or time blocking, to allocate focused periods of time to work on your goals.

7. ESTABLISH ROUTINES:

- Create daily or weekly routines that incorporate goal-related tasks. Consistency in your routines can help maintain focus.

8. SET DEADLINES:

- Establish specific deadlines for your goals and milestones. A sense of urgency can keep you focused on completing tasks within the given timeframes.

9. DEVELOP CONCENTRATION SKILLS:

- Practice techniques to improve your concentration, such as mindfulness meditation or deep work strategies.

10. LIMIT MULTITASKING:

- Avoid multitasking, as it can reduce your ability to focus on one task at a time effectively. Instead, focus on completing one task before moving on to the next.

11. USE TASK LISTS:

- Create to-do lists that outline your daily or weekly tasks. Prioritize tasks and check them off as you complete them.

12. VISUALIZE SUCCESS:

- Regularly visualize yourself achieving your goals. This can help maintain focus on the desired outcome.

13. STAY ORGANIZED:

- Keep your workspace, digital files, and materials organized. Clutter can be distracting and reduce your ability to focus.

14. MAINTAIN WORK-LIFE BALANCE:

- Balance your work on your goals with personal time and relaxation. Burnout can negatively impact your ability to stay focused.

15. SEEK ACCOUNTABILITY:

- Share your goals with an accountability partner or mentor who can help keep you on track and provide encouragement.

16. REVIEW PROGRESS REGULARLY:

- Periodically assess your progress toward your goals. Reviewing your achievements can help maintain motivation and focus.

17. PRACTICE MINDFULNESS:

- Engage in mindfulness practices to enhance your awareness and ability to stay present in the moment. Mindfulness can improve your concentration.

18. LEARN TO SAY NO:

- Be selective about commitments and requests from others. Saying no when necessary allows you to protect your time and focus on your priorities.

19. ADJUST AS NEEDED:

- Be willing to adjust your goals, strategies, or action plans if you encounter unexpected challenges or changes in circumstances. Adaptability supports focus.

20. CELEBRATE ACHIEVEMENTS:

- Celebrate your successes and milestones along the way. Recognizing your accomplishments can boost motivation and reinforce your focus.

Maintaining focus is a skill that can be developed and strengthened over time. By implementing these strategies and consistently practicing them, you can enhance your ability to stay focused on your goals and increase your chances of achieving them.

Lesson 22

MEASUREMENT

Goals allow you to track your progress and evaluate your success objectively.

Measurement is a critical aspect of effective goal setting. It involves defining specific criteria or metrics to assess your progress and determine whether you have successfully achieved your goals. Here's how measurement functions in the goal-setting process:

1. ESTABLISH CLEAR METRICS:

- Define specific and measurable criteria that will determine your progress and success. These metrics should be directly related to the goal and provide a clear indication of achievement.

2. USE QUANTIFIABLE DATA:

- Whenever possible, use quantifiable data or numbers to measure progress and success. For example, if your goal is related to weight loss, use pounds or kilograms lost as a measure.

3. MAKE GOALS TIME-BOUND:

- Incorporate timeframes into your goals to set deadlines for achieving specific milestones or the overall goal. Time-bound goals help measure progress against a set schedule.

4. SET BASELINE MEASURES:

- Establish a baseline or starting point to measure progress from. Knowing where you begin provides context for evaluating your journey

5. TRACK REGULARLY:

- Consistently track your progress toward your goals. This might involve weekly, monthly, or quarterly assessments, depending on the nature of the goal.

6. USE KEY PERFORMANCE INDICATORS (KPIS):

- Identify key performance indicators that are most relevant to your goals. KPIs are specific metrics that directly reflect progress.

7. ADJUST AS NEEDED:

- Be prepared to adjust your metrics or KPIs if circumstances change or if you discover that your initial measures are not effectively tracking your progress.

8. CELEBRATE MILESTONES:

- Celebrate your achievements and milestones along the way. Recognizing progress can motivate you to continue working toward your larger goals.

9. STAY OBJECTIVE:

- Be objective when assessing your progress. Use facts and data rather than subjective feelings or opinions to measure how you are doing.

10. DOCUMENT PROGRESS:

- Keep a record of your measurements and progress over time. This documentation allows you to see trends and patterns in your journey.

11. SEEK FEEDBACK:

- Seek feedback from mentors, coaches, or trusted individuals who can provide an external perspective on your progress and suggest adjustments if necessary

12. ASSESS BARRIERS AND CHALLENGES:

- When you encounter obstacles or setbacks, measure the impact and identify ways to address them effectively. Understanding the challenges can lead to better solutions.

13. COMPARE TO BENCHMARKS:

- Compare your progress to benchmarks or industry standards if applicable. Benchmarking can help you understand where you stand relative to others in your field.

14. PIVOT WHEN NECESSARY:

- If your measurements reveal that your current strategies are not working, be willing to pivot or make significant adjustments to your action plan.

15. STAY CONSISTENT:

- Consistency in measurement is crucial. Use the same metrics and methods throughout the goal-setting process to ensure accurate comparisons.

16. REFLECT AND LEARN:

- Periodically reflect on your progress and the effectiveness of your strategies. Use this information to learn and make improvements.

17. ADJUST GOALS BASED ON MEASUREMENTS:

- If your measurements indicate that your goals need modification, be open to adjusting your goals to align with your current circumstances and priorities.

18. SET NEW GOALS:

- Once you have achieved a goal, use your measurement data to set new goals or to inform future aspirations.

19. MAINTAIN ACCOUNTABILITY:

- Share your measurement data with accountability partners or mentors to maintain transparency and encourage support.

Effective measurement in goal setting not only allows you to track your progress but also provides valuable feedback that can guide your decision-making and strategy adjustments. It helps ensure that you stay on course and make the necessary changes to achieve your objectives successfully.

ACCOUNTABILITY

Sharing your goals with others or keeping them visible can create a sense of responsibility to work toward them.

Setting goals plays a significant role in enhancing accountability. Accountability refers to the responsibility and answerability for one's actions and decisions. Here are the benefits of goal setting in accountability:

CLEAR EXPECTATIONS:

Goals provide a clear and specific target for what needs to be achieved. When goals are well-defined, it's easier to establish expectations and standards for performance and behavior.

MEASURABLE PROGRESS:

Goals often come with metrics or indicators that allow you to measure progress. These measurements provide concrete evidence of whether you're on track or not, which promotes accountability.

DEADLINES:

Goals typically have deadlines or timeframes for achievement. These deadlines create a sense of urgency and help ensure that you remain focused and accountable for completing tasks on time.

OWNERSHIP:

When you set goals, you take ownership of your actions and responsibilities. You become accountable for making choices and decisions that align with your objectives.

MOTIVATION:

Goals provide motivation by giving you a reason to strive for success. Achieving your goals becomes a personal commitment, which motivates you to take action and remain accountable for your progress.

SELF-REFLECTION:

Regularly assessing your progress toward your goals allows you to reflect on your actions and outcomes. This self-reflection promotes accountability as you consider what is and isn't working.

FEEDBACK AND EVALUATION:

Setting goals often involves tracking and evaluating your performance. This feedback loop ensures that you stay accountable by continuously improving and making necessary adjustments.

PRIORITIZATION:

Goals help you prioritize your tasks and focus on what's most important. This ensures that you're accountable for allocating your time and resources to activities that align with your objectives.

COMMUNICATION:

Sharing your goals with others, such as colleagues, mentors, or supervisors, can enhance accountability. When others know about your goals, you're more likely to follow through and report on your progress.

RECOGNITION AND REWARDS:

Achieving your goals often leads to recognition and rewards, which further promote accountability. You're more likely to remain committed when you know there's a positive outcome awaiting you.

COMMITMENT TO SELF:

Setting goals is a commitment to yourself. It represents a promise to achieve certain objectives, which instills a sense of personal integrity and accountability.

In summary, goal setting provides a framework for clear expectations, progress measurement, and accountability. It motivates you to take ownership of your actions, reflect on your performance, and stay committed to your objectives. Accountability is essential for achieving your goals, and goal setting helps create the structure and motivation necessary for success.

ADVANTAGES OF SETTING AND PURSUING GOALS

Goal setting offers numerous benefits in various aspects of life, both personal and professional. Here are some of the key advantages of setting and pursuing goals:

CLARITY AND FOCUS

Goals provide a clear sense of direction and purpose. They help you prioritize your efforts and allocate resources effectively, preventing distractions and wasted time.

Clarity and focus are two fundamental elements of effective goal setting. They work hand in hand to provide a clear direction and unwavering attention to your objectives. Here's how you can cultivate both clarity and focus in your goal-setting process:

CLARITY IN GOAL SETTING:

Define Specific Objectives:

Make sure your goals are specific and well-defined. Clearly articulate what you want to achieve, when you want to achieve it, and why it's important.

Use the SMART Criteria:

Apply the SMART criteria to your goals: Specific, Measurable, Achievable, Relevant, and Time-bound. This framework ensures that your goals are clear and actionable.

Prioritize Goals:

Determine the most important goals and prioritize them based on their significance and alignment with your values and long-term aspirations.

Set Clear Metrics:

Establish specific metrics or criteria for measuring your progress and success. This provides a clear yardstick to evaluate your achievements.

Break Goals into Smaller Steps:

Divide larger goals into smaller, manageable steps or milestones. This not only makes them more achievable but also offers clarity on what needs to be done.

Write Down Your Goals:

Document your goals in writing. Putting them on paper solidifies your commitment and provides a tangible reference.

Visualize Success:

Create a vivid mental image of yourself achieving your goals. Visualization can help you internalize your objectives and make them more concrete.

FOCUS IN GOAL SETTING:

Eliminate Distractions:

Identify common distractions in your environment and work to minimize or eliminate them. This might include turning off notifications, creating a focused workspace, or setting specific work hours.

Set Clear Priorities:

Determine your top priorities and allocate the majority of your time and energy to these essential goals. Avoid spreading yourself too thin by trying to pursue too many objectives simultaneously.

Develop an Action Plan:

Create a detailed action plan that outlines the specific steps required to achieve your goals. Having a clear roadmap helps maintain focus on what needs to be done.

Use Time Management Techniques:

Employ time management techniques like the Pomodoro Technique, time blocking, or the Eisenhower Matrix to structure your work and maintain concentration.

Practice Mindfulness:

Engage in mindfulness practices to enhance your awareness and ability to stay present in the moment. Mindfulness can improve your concentration and reduce mental clutter.

Stay Disciplined:

Cultivate discipline by setting routines and sticking to them. Consistency in your daily habits can help you maintain focus on your goals.

Regularly Review Progress:

Consistently assess your progress toward your goals. Regular reviews help you stay on track and make adjustments as needed.

Avoid Multitasking:

Focus on one task at a time instead of multitasking, which can decrease your effectiveness and focus.

Stay Organized:

Keep your workspace, digital files, and materials organized. Clutter can be distracting and disrupt your concentration.

Stay Motivated:

Maintain your motivation by regularly revisiting your reasons for pursuing your goals. Reconnect with your "why" to reinforce your commitment.

Both clarity and focus are interdependent and critical for achieving your goals. Clarity provides the direction, while focus keeps you on the path toward your objectives. By consciously cultivating these qualities in your goal-setting process, you can enhance your ability to set meaningful goals and work diligently to achieve them.

MOTIVATION

Having specific goals can boost your motivation and enthusiasm. They give you a reason to work harder, persevere through challenges, and stay committed to your objectives.

Motivation is a driving force in the goal-setting process, as it provides the energy and determination needed to work toward and achieve your objectives. Here are key considerations for harnessing motivation in goal setting:

1. SET MEANINGFUL GOALS:

- Choose goals that have personal significance and meaning to you. When your goals align with your values, passions, and long-term aspirations, they become more motivating.

2. UNDERSTAND YOUR "WHY":

- Clearly articulate why each goal is important to you. Understanding the deeper reasons behind your goals can provide a strong sense of purpose and motivation.

3. USE THE SMART CRITERIA:

- Apply the SMART criteria (Specific, Measurable, Achievable, Relevant, Time-bound) to your goals to make them clear and tangible. Well-defined goals are more motivating.

4. BREAK GOALS INTO SMALLER STEPS:

- Divide larger goals into smaller, achievable steps or milestones. Achieving these mini-goals can provide a sense of accomplishment and maintain motivation.

5. VISUALIZE SUCCESS:

- Create a vivid mental image of yourself achieving your goals. Visualization can make your objectives feel more attainable and boost motivation.

6. DEVELOP A PLAN:

- Create a detailed action plan that outlines the specific steps required to achieve your goals. Having a roadmap enhances your sense of direction and motivation.

7. SET DEADLINES:

- Establish specific deadlines for your goals and milestones. Time-bound goals create a sense of urgency and prevent procrastination.

8. FIND ACCOUNTABILITY PARTNERS:

- Share your goals with trusted friends, mentors, or accountability partners who can provide support, encouragement, and accountability.

9. CELEBRATE MILESTONES:

- Acknowledge and celebrate your achievements and milestones along the way. Recognizing progress can boost motivation and morale.

10. STAY POSITIVE:

- Maintain a positive mindset. Focus on your strengths and past successes to build confidence in your ability to achieve your goals.

11. OVERCOME OBSTACLES:

- Identify potential obstacles and develop strategies for overcoming them. A problem-solving mindset can help you stay motivated in the face of challenges.

12. SEEK INTRINSIC MOTIVATION:

- Find internal sources of motivation, such as personal fulfillment, growth, and a sense of purpose. Intrinsic motivation tends to be more sustainable than external rewards.

13. STAY COMMITTED:

- Commit to your goals and remind yourself of your commitment regularly. Staying dedicated, even during challenging times, is a key element of motivation.

14. TRACK PROGRESS:

- Keep a record of your progress. Regularly reviewing your achievements can provide a sense of accomplishment and motivation to keep going.

15. LEARN FROM SETBACKS:

- View setbacks as opportunities for learning and growth. Analyze what went wrong and use the lessons to adjust your approach.

16. SEEK SUPPORT:

- Reach out to supportive communities, forums, or groups that share your goals or interests. Connecting with like-minded individuals can boost motivation.

17. REFLECT AND REEVALUATE:

- Periodically reflect on your progress and reassess your goals. Use this time to adjust your strategies and ensure your goals remain relevant.

18. STAY CONSISTENT:

- Consistency in taking action toward your goals is essential for maintaining motivation. Regular, small steps compound over time.

19. STAY PATIENT:

- Understand that motivation can fluctuate. During periods of low motivation, rely on discipline and commitment to keep moving forward.

20. SET NEW GOALS:

- Once you have achieved a goal, use your newfound motivation to set new goals or to inform future aspirations.

Motivation is not a constant state but rather a dynamic force that can be nurtured and sustained throughout your goal-setting journey. By applying these strategies, you can bolster your motivation and stay committed to achieving your objectives.

MEASURABLE PROGRESS

Goals allow you to measure your progress and success. You can track your achievements, which provides a sense of accomplishment and encourages continued effort.

Measurable progress in goal setting refers to the ability to quantitatively assess and track your advancement toward your goals. Establishing measurable indicators allows you to determine whether you are making headway, staying on course, and ultimately achieving your objectives. Here's how to ensure measurable progress in your goal-setting process:

1. DEFINE CLEAR METRICS:

- Specify precise, quantitative criteria or metrics that will help you assess progress. These metrics should directly relate to the goal and provide a clear measurement of success.

2. USE QUANTIFIABLE DATA:

- Whenever possible, employ quantifiable data or numbers to measure your advancement. For instance, if your goal is related to sales, use revenue figures as a measure of progress.

3. APPLY THE SMART CRITERIA:

- Utilize the SMART criteria (Specific, Measurable, Achievable, Relevant, Time-bound) to make your goals clear and quantifiable. Ensure that your goals are specific enough to be measured

4. SET BASELINE MEASURES:

- Establish a baseline or starting point from which to measure progress. This initial measurement offers context for evaluating how far you've come.

5. TRACK PROGRESS REGULARLY:

- Consistently track your progress toward your goals. This may involve weekly, monthly, or quarterly assessments, depending on the nature of your goal.

6. USE KEY PERFORMANCE INDICATORS (KPIS):

- Identify key performance indicators that are most relevant to your goals. KPIs are specific metrics that directly reflect progress.

7. ADJUST AS NEEDED:

- Be prepared to adjust your metrics or KPIs if circumstances change or if you discover that your initial measures are not effectively tracking progress.

8. CELEBRATE MILESTONES:

- Celebrate your achievements and milestones along the way. Recognizing progress can boost motivation and reinforce positive behaviors.

9. STAY OBJECTIVE:

- Be objective when evaluating your progress. Use facts and data rather than subjective feelings or opinions to measure your accomplishments.

10. DOCUMENT PROGRESS:

- Keep a record of your measurements and progress over time. This documentation allows you to see trends and patterns in your journey.

11. SEEK FEEDBACK:

- Seek feedback from mentors, coaches, or trusted individuals who can provide an external perspective on your progress and suggest adjustments if necessary.

12. ASSESS BARRIERS AND CHALLENGES:

- When you encounter obstacles or setbacks, measure the impact and identify strategies to overcome them effectively. Understanding challenges can lead to better solutions.

13. COMPARE TO BENCHMARKS:

- Compare your progress to benchmarks or industry standards if applicable. Benchmarking can help you understand where you stand relative to others in your field.

14. PIVOT WHEN NECESSARY:

- If your measurements indicate that your current strategies are not working, be willing to pivot or make significant adjustments to your action plan.

15. STAY CONSISTENT:

- Consistency in measurement is crucial. Use the same metrics and methods throughout the goal-setting process to ensure accurate comparisons.

16. REFLECT AND LEARN:

- Periodically reflect on your progress and the effectiveness of your strategies. Use this information to learn and make improvements.

17. ADJUST GOALS BASED ON MEASUREMENTS:

- If your measurements indicate that your goals need modification, be open to adjusting your goals to align with your current circumstances and priorities.

Effective measurement and tracking of progress are essential for staying focused and motivated in your goal-setting journey. By establishing clear metrics and consistently assessing your advancement, you can make informed decisions, stay on course, and take appropriate actions to achieve your objectives successfully.

ACCOUNTABILTY

Sharing your goals with others, or even just writing them down, creates a sense of accountability. You're more likely to work toward your goals when you know others are aware of them.

Accountability is a crucial component of goal setting, and it offers several advantages that can significantly enhance your chances of successfully achieving your objectives. Here are some of the key advantages of accountability in the goal-setting process:

INCREASED MOTIVATION:

When you are held accountable to someone or a group, you are more likely to stay motivated to work toward your goals. The knowledge that others are tracking your progress can provide an extra push to keep you on track.

CLEARER COMMITMENT:

Accountability helps solidify your commitment to your goals. Sharing your goals with someone else or making them public reinforces your dedication to achieving them.

IMPROVED FOCUS:

Knowing that you will be held accountable can help you maintain focus on your goals. You are less likely to get distracted by other tasks or lose sight of your objectives.

STRUCTURED FEEDBACK:

Accountability partners or mentors can provide valuable feedback and insights into your progress. They can offer guidance, suggestions, and constructive criticism to help you stay on the right path.

PROBLEM SOLVING:

When you encounter obstacles or challenges, having someone to be accountable to can be helpful. They may help you brainstorm solutions or provide support during difficult times.

ENHANCED PRODUCTIVITY:

Accountability encourages you to set specific targets and deadlines. This structured approach can lead to increased productivity and efficiency in pursuing your goals.

GREATER RESPONSIBILITY:

Being accountable to someone or a group reinforces your sense of responsibility. You are less likely to make excuses or procrastinate when you know others are watching.

POSITIVE PEER PRESSURE:

Accountability partners or groups can create a positive form of peer pressure. Seeing others making progress on their goals can motivate you to do the same.

CELEBRATING ACHIEVEMENTS:

Accountability partners or groups can celebrate your achievements and milestones with you. This recognition can boost your morale and sense of accomplishment.

SUPPORT SYSTEM:

Accountability partners or groups can serve as a support system during challenging times. They can provide encouragement, advice, and assistance when needed.

CONSISTENCY:

Regular check-ins and reporting to an accountability partner or group help establish a consistent routine for tracking your progress. Consistency is essential for goal achievement.

MEASURABLE PROGRESS:

Accountability allows for the measurement of your progress, which provides valuable data to assess how you are doing and make necessary adjustments.

GOAL COMPLETION:

Ultimately, accountability increases the likelihood of achieving your goals. When you are accountable to someone else, you are more likely to follow through on your commitments.

LEARNING OPPORTUNITIES:

Accountability provides opportunities for learning and personal growth. Feedback from accountability partners or groups can help you refine your strategies and become a better goal-setter and achiever.

LONG-TERM SUCCESS:

Establishing accountability practices can lead to long-term success in goal setting. The discipline and habits you develop can be applied to future goals, creating a cycle of achievement.

In summary, accountability in goal setting can serve as a powerful motivator, provide valuable support and feedback, and increase your commitment and focus. By leveraging the advantages of accountability, you can enhance your ability to set and achieve meaningful objectives in various aspects of your life.

Lesson 28

BETTER DECISION MAKING

Goals help you make decisions that align with your desired outcomes. When faced with choices, you can assess which option will bring you closer to your goals

Better decision-making is a crucial advantage that stems from effective goal setting. When you set clear and meaningful goals, it can significantly improve your decision-making processes in several ways:

CLEAR DIRECTION:

Well-defined goals provide you with a clear sense of direction. When you know what you want to achieve, it becomes easier to make decisions that align with your objectives and avoid choices that lead you off course.

PRIORITIZATION:

Goal setting encourages you to prioritize your tasks and activities. You can make decisions based on which actions will have the most significant impact on your goals, helping you allocate your time and resources more effectively.

FOCUSED DECISION-MAKING:

With goals in mind, you can make more focused decisions. Instead of being overwhelmed by choices, you can filter options based on whether they contribute to or detract from your goals.

REDUCED PROCRASTINATION:

Clear goals can reduce procrastination because they provide a sense of urgency. When you have specific deadlines or milestones to meet, it's easier to make decisions that move you closer to those targets.

BETTER TIME MANAGEMENT:

Goal setting encourages better time management skills. You're more likely to make decisions about how to use your time wisely when you have a clear understanding of your priorities and deadlines.

IMPROVED RESOURCE ALLOCATION:

Goal setting helps you allocate your resources, including time, money, and energy, more efficiently. You can make decisions about where to invest your resources to achieve the most significant impact on your goals.

CONFLICT RESOLUTION:

Goals can help in conflict resolution. When faced with a decision that involves potential conflicts or trade-offs, you can refer back to your goals to guide your choices and find solutions that align with your objectives.

ENHANCED FOCUS ON LONG-TERM OBJECTIVES:

Effective goal setting encourages a long-term perspective. Instead of making short-sighted decisions, you're more likely to consider the long-term consequences and benefits of your choices.

RISK ASSESSMENT:

Goals prompt you to assess risks and rewards. When making decisions, you can evaluate whether a particular choice aligns with your risk tolerance and the potential impact on your goals.

BOOSTED CONFIDENCE:

Setting and achieving goals can boost your confidence in decision-making. Successes along the way can provide evidence that your choices are leading you in the right direction.

ALIGNMENT WITH VALUES:

Goal setting often involves aligning your goals with your core values and principles. This ensures that your decisions are consistent with your personal beliefs and ethics.

ACCOUNTABILITY:

When you share your goals with others or have an accountability partner, you have someone to hold you accountable for your decisions. This added layer of responsibility can influence your choices positively.

ADAPTABILITY:

While goals provide direction, they also encourage adaptability. You become more open to adjusting your decisions and strategies when you encounter unforeseen challenges or opportunities, ensuring that you stay on the path to your goals.

REFLECTIVE PRACTICE:

Goal setting encourages reflective practice. Regularly reviewing your goals and progress prompts you to reflect on past decisions, learn from them, and apply those lessons to future choices.

PERSONAL GROWTH:

Pursuing goals often involves personal growth and development. As you make decisions that support your goals, you can grow in various aspects of your life, such as skills, knowledge, and self-awareness.

In essence, effective goal setting provides a framework for making more deliberate, focused, and informed decisions. It guides your choices toward actions that are aligned with your aspirations and priorities, ultimately leading to greater success and fulfillment.

Lesson 29

TIME MANAGEMENT

Setting deadlines and timeframes for your goals promotes effective time management. You learn to allocate your time wisely and avoid procrastination

Effective time management is essential for successful goal setting and offers several advantages that can significantly enhance your ability to achieve your objectives. Here are the key advantages of time management in goal setting:

PRIORITIZATION:

Time management helps you identify and prioritize tasks and activities that are most aligned with your goals. It enables you to allocate your time to the most important and high-impact actions.

FOCUS ON GOALS:

Good time management ensures that you dedicate sufficient time and attention to your goals. It helps you avoid distractions and stay focused on tasks that move you closer to your objectives.

EFFICIENCY:

Time management techniques and strategies improve your efficiency and productivity. You can accomplish more in less time, allowing you to make progress toward your goals at a faster pace.

EFFECTIVE PLANNING:

Time management involves planning and scheduling your tasks. This planning ensures that you have a clear roadmap for achieving your goals, making it easier to stay on track.

REDUCED PROCRASTINATION:

Procrastination is a common obstacle to goal achievement. Time management helps you overcome procrastination by breaking tasks into manageable chunks and setting deadlines.

INCREASED SELF-DISCIPLINE:

Effective time management requires discipline and self-control. These qualities are essential for consistently taking the necessary actions to reach your goals.

BETTER DECISION-MAKING:

Time management allows you to make informed decisions about how to use your time wisely. You can weigh the benefits of different tasks against your goals and choose accordingly.

TIME FOR REFLECTION:

Time management provides space for reflection. Regularly reviewing your goals and progress allows you to make adjustments and refine your strategies as needed.

STRESS REDUCTION:

Poor time management can lead to stress and overwhelm. By managing your time effectively, you can reduce stress and maintain a healthier work-life balance, which is crucial for long-term goal pursuit.

INCREASED ACCOUNTABILITY:

When you allocate specific time slots for tasks related to your goals, you become more accountable to yourself. This accountability helps ensure that you consistently work toward your objectives.

OPTIMAL RESOURCE ALLOCATION:

Effective time management helps you allocate your resources, including time, energy, and money, optimally. You can invest these resources in activities that have the greatest impact on your goals.

IMPROVED ORGANIZATION:

Organizing your tasks and activities is a key component of time management. This organization ensures that you have a clear structure for pursuing your goals.

BETTER WORK-LIFE BALANCE:

Time management encourages a balance between work, personal life, and goal pursuit. Achieving this balance is vital for well-being and long-term success.

INCREASED CONFIDENCE:

As you accomplish tasks and make progress toward your goals through effective time management, your confidence grows. This increased self-assurance can positively impact your goal-setting journey.

ADAPTABILITY:

Time management strategies promote adaptability. When you encounter unexpected challenges or opportunities, effective time management allows you to adjust your schedule and priorities while still working toward your goals.

CONSISTENCY:

Consistency is essential for achieving long-term goals. Time management helps you develop consistent habits and routines, ensuring that you take regular steps toward your objectives.

TIME FOR PERSONAL GROWTH:

Time management creates space for personal growth and development. You can allocate time for learning, skill-building, and self-improvement, all of which can enhance your ability to achieve your goals.

In summary, time management is a critical component of goal setting that empowers you to make the most of your time, prioritize effectively, and consistently take action toward your objectives. It maximizes your productivity, reduces stress, and increases your chances of successfully achieving your goals.

INCREASED RESILIENCE

Pursuing goals often involves overcoming obstacles and setbacks. This can build resilience and the ability to bounce back from failures.

Increasing resilience in the context of goal setting can have several advantages that enhance your ability to set and achieve your objectives effectively.

Resilience refers to the capacity to bounce back from setbacks, adapt to challenges, and maintain motivation in the face of adversity. Here are the advantages of increasing resilience in goal setting:

BETTER COPING WITH SETBACKS:

Resilience equips you with the mental and emotional strength to cope with setbacks and failures. When pursuing goals, you are likely to encounter obstacles and disappointments. Resilience helps you bounce back, learn from these experiences, and continue progressing.

SUSTAINED MOTIVATION:

Resilient individuals are better at maintaining motivation and commitment to their goals, even when facing difficulties. This persistence is crucial for long-term goal achievement, as it prevents discouragement and gives you the stamina to keep going.

ENHANCED PROBLEM-SOLVING SKILLS:

Resilience fosters adaptability and problem-solving abilities. When challenges arise, you are more likely to approach them with a flexible mindset, seeking creative solutions and alternatives to stay on track toward your goals.

INCREASED STRESS MANAGEMENT:

Setting and pursuing goals can be stressful, especially when you encounter unexpected obstacles. Resilience helps you manage stress more effectively, reducing its negative impact on your physical and mental well-being.

EMOTIONAL REGULATION:

Resilience is associated with better emotional regulation. This skill is valuable when goal setting, as it helps you stay focused and make rational decisions, even when facing emotional challenges.

OPTIMISM AND POSITIVE OUTLOOK:

Resilient individuals tend to maintain an optimistic and positive outlook. This attitude can be a significant asset when working toward your goals, as it fosters a belief in your ability to overcome obstacles and achieve success.

ADAPTATION TO CHANGE:

Goal-setting journeys often require adaptation to changing circumstances and priorities. Resilience enables you to navigate transitions and adjust your goals and strategies when necessary.

IMPROVED DECISION-MAKING:

Resilient individuals are better equipped to make informed decisions, even in high-pressure situations. This skill can help you make sound choices that align with your goals, even when facing uncertainty.

INCREASED SELF-EFFICACY:

Resilience contributes to higher self-efficacy—the belief in your ability to accomplish your goals. When you have confidence in your resilience, you are more likely to take on challenging goals and persevere.

GREATER ACCEPTANCE OF IMPERFECTION:

Resilience helps you accept that setbacks and imperfections are a natural part of the goal-setting process. You are less likely to be discouraged by mistakes and more inclined to view them as opportunities for growth.

ENHANCED RELATIONSHIPS:

Resilient individuals tend to have better interpersonal relationships. These connections can provide support, encouragement, and accountability as you work toward your goals.

INCREASED OVERALL WELL-BEING:

Building resilience contributes to overall well-being. When you feel mentally and emotionally strong, you are better equipped to pursue your goals with enthusiasm and dedication.

LONG-TERM SUCCESS:

Resilience is a key factor in achieving long-term success. It helps you weather the ups and downs of your journey and maintain momentum over time.

ROLE MODELING:

Demonstrating resilience in goal setting can inspire others around you. Your ability to bounce back from setbacks can serve as an example and encourage others to pursue their goals with determination.

In summary, increasing resilience in goal setting offers numerous advantages that can significantly enhance your ability to overcome challenges, maintain motivation, and ultimately achieve your objectives. Resilience equips you with the mental and emotional strength needed to navigate the often winding and challenging path of goal pursuit.

PERSONAL GROWTH

- Setting and achieving goals can lead to personal growth and development. You acquire new skills, gain knowledge, and expand your capabilities in the process.

Personal growth is intimately connected with goal setting and offers numerous advantages that can significantly enhance your ability to set and achieve your objectives. Here are the advantages of personal growth in the context of goal setting:

ENHANCED SELF-AWARENESS:

Pursuing personal growth encourages self-reflection and self-awareness. This deeper understanding of yourself helps you set goals that align with your values, passions, and strengths.

INCREASED MOTIVATION:

Personal growth often involves setting goals for self-improvement, which can boost your motivation. Achieving personal growth milestones can serve as a powerful motivator to continue setting and pursuing new goals.

IMPROVED GOAL-SETTING SKILLS:

As you engage in personal growth, you become more adept at setting clear, specific, and achievable goals. This skill enhances your ability to articulate your aspirations and create effective action plans.

ENHANCED ADAPTABILITY:

Personal growth fosters adaptability and resilience. You become better at navigating obstacles, adjusting to changing circumstances, and staying committed to your goals despite setbacks.

EXPANDED SKILL SET:

Pursuing personal growth often involves acquiring new skills and knowledge. These additional capabilities can be directly applied to help you achieve your goals more effectively.

INCREASED CONFIDENCE:

As you grow personally, you gain confidence in your abilities and potential. This heightened self-assurance can boost your belief in your capacity to achieve challenging goals.

GREATER CLARITY OF PURPOSE:

Personal growth helps you gain clarity about your life's purpose and direction. This clarity enables you to set more meaningful and purpose-driven goals.

ENHANCED PROBLEM-SOLVING SKILLS:

Personal growth often includes developing problem-solving and critical thinking skills. These skills are valuable when you encounter obstacles or challenges in your goal-setting journey.

POSITIVE MINDSET:

Personal growth often involves cultivating a positive mindset. A positive attitude can help you stay motivated, maintain optimism, and persevere through difficulties while pursuing your goals.

EMOTIONAL INTELLIGENCE:

Personal growth can lead to increased emotional intelligence, which is valuable in interpersonal relationships and when dealing with emotions that arise during the goal-setting process.

IMPROVED TIME MANAGEMENT:

Personal growth often includes developing time management and organizational skills. These skills are essential for effectively managing your time when working toward your goals.

BETTER DECISION-MAKING:

Personal growth encourages better decision-making by fostering self-awareness, emotional intelligence, and a deeper understanding of your values and priorities.

ENHANCED COMMUNICATION SKILLS:

As you grow personally, your communication skills tend to improve. Effective communication is crucial when collaborating with others or seeking support for your goals.

INCREASED RESILIENCE:

Personal growth typically leads to increased resilience. A resilient mindset can help you bounce back from setbacks and continue pursuing your goals with determination.

HEALTH AND WELL-BEING:

Many aspects of personal growth, such as adopting healthier habits and managing stress, can contribute to improved physical and mental well-being. A healthy body and mind are essential for sustained goal pursuit.

POSITIVE HABITS AND ROUTINES:

Personal growth often involves the development of positive habits and routines that can support your goal-setting efforts. These habits can include daily practices that enhance productivity, creativity, and focus.

LIFELONG LEARNING:

Personal growth encourages a commitment to lifelong learning and self-improvement. This mindset can drive your ongoing development and adaptation to new goals and challenges.

POSITIVE INFLUENCE ON OTHERS:

Your personal growth journey can inspire and positively influence others around you, motivating them to embark on their own journeys of self-improvement and goal achievement.

OVERALL LIFE SATISFACTION:

Personal growth contributes to overall life satisfaction and a sense of fulfillment. As you evolve and grow, you are likely to experience greater contentment and happiness, which can positively impact your goal-setting efforts.

In summary, personal growth and goal setting are intertwined, with personal growth acting as a powerful catalyst for setting and achieving meaningful objectives. The advantages of personal growth include improved self-awareness, motivation, goal-setting skills, adaptability, and overall well-being, all of which enhance your ability to pursue and accomplish your goals successfully.

ENHANCED SELF - ESTEEM

- Achieving your goals can boost your self-esteem and self-confidence. You gain a sense of pride and self-worth when you see the results of your efforts.

Enhancing self-esteem in the goal-setting process can have several advantages that significantly improve your ability to set and achieve your objectives. Self-esteem refers to your overall sense of self-worth and confidence in your abilities. Here are the advantages of enhancing self-esteem in the context of goal setting:

INCREASED CONFIDENCE:

Improved self-esteem boosts your confidence in your ability to set and achieve goals. You believe in yourself more, which can positively impact your motivation and determination.

POSITIVE SELF-IMAGE:

A healthy self-esteem fosters a positive self-image. When you feel good about yourself, you are more likely to set ambitious, high-value goals that align with your true potential.

RISK-TAKING:

Higher self-esteem often leads to a willingness to take calculated risks. You are more likely to step out of your comfort zone and pursue challenging goals because you have faith in your capacity to handle uncertainty.

REDUCED FEAR OF FAILURE:

Enhanced self-esteem can reduce the fear of failure. You are less likely to be deterred by setbacks or fear of criticism, allowing you to persevere in the face of adversity.

INCREASED RESILIENCE:

A strong sense of self-esteem can make you more resilient. You are better equipped to bounce back from failures or setbacks and maintain your self-belief throughout your goal-setting journey.

POSITIVE SELF-TALK:

With higher self-esteem, you tend to engage in more positive self-talk. This internal dialogue can boost your self-confidence and motivation, reinforcing your commitment to your goals.

SETTING AMBITIOUS GOALS:

When you believe in your abilities, you are more likely to set ambitious, meaningful goals. This can lead to more significant personal and professional achievements.

EFFECTIVE PROBLEM-SOLVING:

Higher self-esteem can improve your problem-solving skills. You are more likely to approach challenges with a solutions-oriented mindset, seeking constructive ways to overcome obstacles.

IMPROVED DECISION-MAKING:

Enhanced self-esteem can lead to better decision-making. You are more likely to make choices that align with your values and long-term goals, rather than settling for less.

REDUCED SELF-DOUBT:

Improved self-esteem diminishes self-doubt. You are less likely to second-guess yourself, which can result in more decisive and assertive actions toward your goals.

OPTIMISM:

A positive self-esteem often correlates with a more optimistic outlook on life. Optimism can help you maintain a positive attitude, even in the face of challenges, making it easier to stay committed to your goals.

GREATER SELF-RELIANCE:

Enhanced self-esteem encourages self-reliance. You rely more on your own abilities and judgment, which can lead to greater autonomy in setting and pursuing your goals.

STRONGER INTERPERSONAL RELATIONSHIPS:

Higher self-esteem can positively impact your relationships. You are more likely to engage in healthy, assertive communication, seek support when needed, and foster positive relationships with others who share your goals.

INCREASED GOAL COMMITMENT:

When you believe in yourself and your abilities, you are more committed to your goals. This commitment can translate into a greater willingness to invest time, effort, and resources in goal pursuit.

BETTER OVERALL WELL-BEING:

Enhanced self-esteem contributes to improved overall well-being. A positive self-concept can lead to increased happiness, self-satisfaction, and life fulfillment, all of which can positively influence your goal-setting efforts.

ROLE MODELING:

Your enhanced self-esteem can serve as a positive example for others. Your self-assuredness can inspire those around you to set and pursue their own goals with confidence.

In summary, enhancing self-esteem can be a powerful catalyst for successful goal setting. It boosts your confidence, reduces self-doubt, encourages ambition, and fosters resilience, all of which contribute to a more positive and effective goal-setting process.

IMPROVED WELL-BEING

- Accomplishing meaningful goals can contribute to a sense of fulfillment and overall well-being. It can reduce stress and increase overall life satisfaction.

Improved well-being plays a vital role in goal setting, and it offers several advantages that can significantly enhance your ability to set and achieve your objectives. Well-being encompasses physical, mental, and emotional health, as well as overall life satisfaction. Here are the advantages of improved well-being in the context of goal setting:

INCREASED MOTIVATION:

Improved well-being can boost your motivation to set and pursue goals. When you feel physically and mentally well, you are more likely to have the energy and enthusiasm needed for goal achievement.

OPTIMAL PHYSICAL HEALTH:

A focus on well-being often includes adopting healthier lifestyle habits, such as regular exercise and a balanced diet. Physical health and vitality are essential for sustained goal pursuit.

ENHANCED MENTAL HEALTH:

Prioritizing well-being can lead to improved mental health. Reduced stress, anxiety, and depression can positively impact your ability to set clear goals and stay focused on them.

BETTER EMOTIONAL RESILIENCE:

Improved well-being can enhance your emotional resilience. You are better equipped to manage emotions, cope with setbacks, and maintain a positive attitude during your goal-setting journey.

GREATER FOCUS AND CONCENTRATION:

Good well-being supports enhanced cognitive function. This means improved focus, concentration, and mental clarity, which are crucial for effective goal setting and execution.

ENHANCED CREATIVITY:

A balanced and healthy mind often leads to increased creativity. Creative thinking can help you come up with innovative solutions and approaches to achieving your goals.

STRESS REDUCTION:

Prioritizing well-being includes stress management strategies. Reducing stress levels is vital for maintaining your physical and mental health during goal pursuit.

BETTER SLEEP PATTERNS:

Well-being practices often promote healthy sleep patterns. Quality sleep is essential for cognitive function, mood regulation, and overall energy levels, which are all relevant to goal setting.

POSITIVE MINDSET:

Improved well-being is associated with a more positive mindset. A positive attitude can boost your belief in your ability to achieve your goals, even in the face of challenges.

RESILIENCE TO SETBACKS:

Good well-being equips you with the resilience needed to bounce back from setbacks. You are more likely to view setbacks as opportunities for growth rather than insurmountable obstacles.

ENHANCED RELATIONSHIPS:

A focus on well-being can lead to healthier interpersonal relationships. Positive social connections can provide support, encouragement, and accountability for your goals.

IMPROVED TIME MANAGEMENT:

Well-being practices often include time management and organization skills. These skills are essential for effectively allocating your time toward your goals.

BALANCED LIFE:

Prioritizing well-being encourages a balanced life. A healthy work-life balance ensures that you have the time and energy to dedicate to your personal and professional goals.

INCREASED CONFIDENCE:

When you are physically and mentally well, your self-confidence tends to be higher. This increased confidence can positively impact your belief in your ability to achieve your goals.

GREATER LIFE SATISFACTION:

Improved well-being contributes to overall life satisfaction. Feeling content and fulfilled in various aspects of your life can provide a positive foundation for setting and achieving meaningful goals.

ROLE MODELING:

Your commitment to well-being can serve as a positive example for others. Your healthy habits and choices can inspire those around you to prioritize their own well-being and pursue their goals with vigor.

LONG-TERM SUCCESS:

Good well-being practices are essential for achieving long-term success. They help you maintain the physical and mental resilience needed for sustained goal pursuit.

In summary, improved well-being is a foundation for successful goal setting. It provides the physical and mental resources necessary for motivation, focus, resilience, and overall life satisfaction, all of which contribute to a more effective and fulfilling goal-setting process.

POSITIVE HABITS

- Working toward goals often involves developing positive habits and routines. These habits can have long-lasting benefits in various areas of your life.

Developing positive habits is a powerful strategy in goal setting and offers several advantages that can significantly enhance your ability to set and achieve your objectives. Positive habits provide structure, consistency, and a framework for success. Here are the advantages of cultivating positive habits in the context of goal setting:

CONSISTENCY:

Positive habits create a consistent routine, making it easier to stay on track with your goals. Consistency is crucial for long-term success and progress.

INCREASED PRODUCTIVITY:

Habits help you streamline your actions, making you more efficient and productive in pursuing your goals. You can accomplish more in less time by automating certain tasks.

IMPROVED FOCUS:

Habits help you maintain focus on your goals by reducing distractions and minimizing decision fatigue. When something becomes a habit, you don't have to think about it as much, freeing up mental energy for other tasks.

TIME MANAGEMENT:

Positive habits often involve effective time management practices. These habits help you allocate your time efficiently to tasks that align with your goals.

GOAL ALIGNMENT:

Habits can be directly aligned with your goals. By developing habits that support your objectives, you ensure that you consistently work toward achieving them.

SELF-DISCIPLINE:

Cultivating positive habits requires self-discipline and willpower. These qualities are essential for staying committed to your goals, especially when faced with challenges.

REDUCTION OF PROCRASTINATION:

Positive habits help combat procrastination by creating a structured approach to tasks. You are less likely to put things off when they are part of your daily routine.

STRESS REDUCTION:

Habits can reduce stress by providing a sense of control and predictability in your life. When you have habits in place, you know what to expect and how to manage your time effectively.

PERSONAL GROWTH:

Positive habits often lead to personal growth and development. As you consistently engage in these habits, you can acquire new skills, knowledge, and experiences that enhance your abilities.

CONFIDENCE BUILDING:

Successfully maintaining positive habits can boost your self-confidence. Achieving small wins every day reinforces your belief in your ability to achieve more significant goals.

ADAPTABILITY:

While habits provide structure, they can also be adaptable. You can adjust your habits as needed to accommodate changing circumstances or priorities.

EFFICIENCY:

Positive habits make you more efficient in accomplishing tasks, reducing wasted time and effort. This efficiency allows you to make the most of your resources.

POSITIVE FEEDBACK LOOP:

Developing and maintaining positive habits creates a positive feedback loop. As you see progress and positive results, it reinforces your commitment to your goals and habits.

LONG-TERM SUCCESS:

Habits contribute to long-term success by helping you establish a sustainable routine. Over time, these habits can lead to significant accomplishments.

ACCOUNTABILITY:

Your habits can serve as a form of self-accountability. When you consistently engage in habits that support your goals, you hold yourself responsible for your progress.

RITUALS AND CUES:

Positive habits often have associated rituals or cues that signal the beginning or end of a task. These cues help you transition smoothly between different activities in your goal-setting journey.

IMPROVED HEALTH AND WELL-BEING:

Many positive habits are related to health and well-being, such as exercise, healthy eating, and stress management. These habits can positively impact your physical and mental health, enhancing your overall well-being.

SUSTAINABILITY:

Positive habits are sustainable in the long run. They become a natural part of your daily life, making it easier to maintain your progress and continue working toward your goals.

In summary, cultivating positive habits is a valuable strategy in goal setting. These habits provide structure, consistency, and discipline, which are essential for achieving your objectives. By incorporating positive habits into your routine, you can significantly enhance your ability to make progress and attain success in various aspects of your life.

LONG TERM VISION

- Goals help you think about the bigger picture and where you want to be in the future. They encourage you to set long-term objectives and plan for the future.

Having a long-term vision in goal setting offers several advantages that can significantly enhance your ability to set and achieve your objectives. A long-term vision refers to a clear and inspiring picture of your desired future, often encompassing goals and aspirations that extend beyond the immediate future. Here are the advantages of incorporating a long-term vision into your goal-setting process:

CLARITY OF PURPOSE:

A long-term vision provides clarity about your life's purpose and direction. It helps you understand what truly matters to you and why you are pursuing specific goals.

MOTIVATION:

A compelling long-term vision serves as a powerful source of motivation. It provides a deeper, intrinsic reason for setting and pursuing goals, which can help you stay committed even when faced with obstacles.

GOAL ALIGNMENT:

Your long-term vision guides the setting of short-term and medium-term goals. It ensures that your goals are aligned with your overarching life vision, creating a sense of coherence and meaning.

RESILIENCE:

A long-term vision fosters resilience. When setbacks occur, you can draw strength from your vision, knowing that the journey toward your ultimate goals involves ups and downs.

BIG-PICTURE THINKING:

A long-term vision encourages big-picture thinking. It helps you see beyond immediate concerns and prioritize long-range objectives, which can lead to more impactful and sustainable goals.

STRATEGIC PLANNING:

Long-term visions inform strategic planning. You can create a roadmap that outlines the steps, milestones, and resources required to bring your vision to fruition.

FOCUS ON VALUES:

A long-term vision often reflects your core values and principles. This focus on values ensures that your goals are consistent with your beliefs and ethics.

LONG-TERM SATISFACTION:

Pursuing a long-term vision can lead to long-term satisfaction and fulfillment. It encourages you to invest in goals that provide lasting happiness and life satisfaction.

TIME PERSPECTIVE:

A long-term vision shifts your time perspective from short-term to long-term. This shift can help you make choices and decisions that prioritize long-term benefits over immediate gratification.

CREATIVITY AND INNOVATION:

Long-term visions often require creative thinking and innovation. You are more likely to explore new ideas and approaches to achieve your long-range goals.

PERSONAL GROWTH:

A long-term vision fosters personal growth and development. As you work toward your vision, you may acquire new skills, knowledge, and experiences that contribute to your growth.

BETTER DECISION-MAKING:

A long-term vision guides decision-making. When faced with choices, you can evaluate them based on whether they align with your vision and long-term goals.

ADAPTABILITY:

Long-term visions encourage adaptability. While the vision itself remains stable, the strategies and tactics for achieving it can be adjusted to accommodate changing circumstances.

LEGACY:

Your long-term vision can encompass the legacy you want to leave behind. This can inspire you to work on goals that have a lasting impact on your community, industry, or the world.

POSITIVE INFLUENCE ON OTHERS:

Sharing your long-term vision can inspire and positively influence others. It can encourage those around you to set their own long-range goals and pursue meaningful aspirations.

SENSE OF ACHIEVEMENT:

Achieving long-term goals associated with your vision provides a profound sense of achievement and fulfillment. These accomplishments can be highly rewarding and fulfilling.

LIFE SATISFACTION:

A long-term vision contributes to overall life satisfaction. It ensures that you are working toward a future that aligns with your deepest desires and aspirations.

In summary, a long-term vision is a powerful tool in goal setting that provides direction, motivation, and purpose. It helps you set meaningful and enduring goals, fosters resilience, encourages strategic planning, and contributes to personal growth and satisfaction. Integrating a long-term vision into your goal-setting process can lead to a more fulfilling and purpose-driven life.

ENHANCED FOCUS ON PRIORITIES

- Goals help you determine what truly matters to you and what you want to prioritize in your life.

Enhancing your focus on priorities in goal setting offers several advantages that can significantly improve your ability to set and achieve your objectives. Prioritization involves identifying the most important goals and tasks and allocating resources accordingly. Here are the advantages of prioritizing in the context of goal setting:

CLARITY:

Prioritization provides clarity about what truly matters. It helps you identify and focus on the goals that align most closely with your values, vision, and long-term objectives.

EFFICIENCY:

By concentrating your efforts on high-priority goals, you become more efficient in achieving meaningful outcomes. You can allocate your time, energy, and resources where they have the greatest impact.

FOCUS:

Prioritizing goals enhances your ability to stay focused. It reduces distractions and prevents you from spreading yourself too thin across multiple objectives, ensuring that you make meaningful progress.

EFFECTIVE RESOURCE ALLOCATION:

Prioritization enables you to allocate resources, including time, money, and effort, more effectively. You invest these resources where they are most likely to yield the desired results.

GOAL ALIGNMENT:

Prioritization ensures that your goals are aligned with your overarching vision and purpose. It creates synergy between your short-term and long-term objectives.

INCREASED PRODUCTIVITY:

By concentrating on high-priority goals, you can accomplish more in less time. This increased productivity allows you to make consistent progress toward your objectives.

STRESS REDUCTION:

Prioritization can reduce stress by helping you manage your workload effectively. When you have a clear sense of what to focus on, you can avoid the overwhelm that often comes from juggling too many tasks

ENHANCED DECISION-MAKING:

Prioritization improves decision-making. You can evaluate options and choices based on their alignment with your top priorities, making it easier to make informed decisions.

IMPROVED TIME MANAGEMENT:

Prioritizing goals is a cornerstone of effective time management. It helps you allocate your time wisely, ensuring that you spend it on tasks that matter most.

GOAL ACHIEVEMENT:

Prioritization increases the likelihood of achieving your most important goals. By dedicating your efforts to high-priority objectives, you are more likely to see significant results.

ALIGNMENT WITH VALUES:

Prioritization ensures that your actions align with your values. It prevents you from pursuing goals that may conflict with your core principles.

ADAPTABILITY:

Prioritization allows for adaptability. When circumstances change or new opportunities arise, you can adjust your priorities while still maintaining focus on your most critical objectives.

POSITIVE IMPACT:

High-priority goals often have a more significant positive impact on your life and the lives of others. Prioritization enables you to contribute meaningfully to your community, industry, or the world.

LONG-TERM SUCCESS:

Prioritizing goals contributes to long-term success. It ensures that you are consistently working toward the objectives that have the greatest potential to shape your future.

SATISFACTION AND FULFILLMENT:

Accomplishing high-priority goals is inherently satisfying and fulfilling. The sense of achievement and progress can boost your overall satisfaction and well-being.

LEGACY BUILDING:

Prioritizing goals allows you to focus on goals that contribute to your desired legacy. You can work on objectives that leave a lasting impact on future generations or your chosen field.

POSITIVE INFLUENCE ON OTHERS:

When you prioritize effectively, you can inspire and positively influence others to do the same. Your commitment to priorities can encourage those around you to set and pursue their own meaningful goals.

In summary, enhancing your focus on priorities in goal setting is a strategic approach that yields numerous advantages.

It helps you maintain clarity, efficiency, and focus, ensures effective resource allocation, reduces stress, and increases the likelihood of goal achievement. Prioritization is a fundamental principle for success in goal setting and life in general.

INCREASED PRODUCTIVITY

- With clear goals, you become more productive because you have a sense of purpose and direction in your daily tasks.

Increasing productivity in the context of goal setting offers several advantages that can significantly enhance your ability to set and achieve your objectives. Productivity involves efficiently using your time, energy, and resources to accomplish tasks and goals. Here are the advantages of increasing productivity in goal setting:

EFFICIENT RESOURCE ALLOCATION:

Increased productivity helps you allocate your time, energy, and resources more efficiently to work on your goals. You can maximize the impact of your efforts.

TIME MANAGEMENT:

Productivity techniques and habits improve your time management skills. You can prioritize tasks and allocate sufficient time to work on your goals effectively.

HIGHER OUTPUT:

Enhanced productivity often results in higher output and achievement of tasks and goals. You can complete more work in less time, leading to increased progress.

CONSISTENCY:

Productivity practices encourage consistency in your work. This consistency is essential for making steady progress toward your goals.

FOCUSED EFFORT:

Increased productivity helps you maintain focus on the most important tasks related to your goals. You can avoid distractions and stay on track.

GOAL ALIGNMENT:

Productivity techniques align your efforts with your goals. You can identify and work on tasks that directly contribute to goal achievement.

REDUCED PROCRASTINATION:

Productivity strategies can help combat procrastination. You are more likely to tackle tasks and make progress on your goals instead of putting them off.

STRESS REDUCTION:

Efficiently managing your time and tasks can reduce stress. You can avoid the anxiety that comes from feeling overwhelmed or falling behind on your goals.

EFFECTIVE PLANNING:

Productivity practices often involve effective planning and organization. You can create detailed action plans that outline the steps required to achieve your goals.

BETTER DECISION-MAKING:

Productivity habits improve decision-making. When you have a clear understanding of your goals and priorities, you can make more informed choices.

IMPROVED FOCUS:

Productivity techniques enhance your ability to concentrate on tasks. You can work with greater focus and attention, leading to better results.

OPTIMAL USE OF ENERGY:

Increased productivity ensures that you use your energy effectively. You can match your energy levels with tasks that require the most effort and concentration.

GOAL PROGRESS TRACKING:

Productivity methods often involve tracking progress and measuring results. You can monitor how close you are to achieving your goals and make adjustments as needed.

ADAPTABILITY:

Productivity techniques help you adapt to changes and challenges. You can adjust your strategies and priorities while maintaining progress toward your goals.

POSITIVE HABITS:

Productivity practices often lead to the development of positive habits. These habits can support your goal-setting efforts and lead to sustained progress.

PERSONAL GROWTH:

As you increase your productivity, you may acquire new skills, knowledge, and experiences that contribute to personal growth and development.

GOAL ACHIEVEMENT:

Ultimately, increased productivity increases the likelihood of achieving your goals. You can accomplish more in less time, allowing you to make significant strides toward your objectives.

GREATER SATISFACTION:

Successfully implementing productivity techniques can lead to greater satisfaction and a sense of accomplishment. You can take pride in your ability to manage your time and make progress on your goals.

In summary, increasing productivity is a valuable strategy in goal setting that offers numerous advantages. It helps you allocate resources efficiently, manage time effectively, stay focused, reduce stress, and make consistent progress toward your objectives. By enhancing your productivity, you can significantly improve your chances of achieving your goals and realizing your desired outcomes.

Lesson 38

FINANCIAL SECURITY

- Setting financial goals, such as saving or investing, can lead to increased financial security and independence.

Financial security plays a pivotal role in goal setting and offers several advantages that can significantly enhance your ability to set and achieve your objectives. Having financial stability and security provides a strong foundation for pursuing both short-term and long-term goals. Here are the advantages of financial security in the context of goal setting:

REDUCED STRESS:

Financial security reduces the stress associated with financial uncertainty. When you have a stable financial situation, you can focus more on your goals and less on immediate financial concerns.

FREEDOM TO CHOOSE:

Financial security provides you with the freedom to choose the goals that matter most to you, rather than being constrained by financial limitations.

EXPANDED OPPORTUNITIES:

With financial security, you have access to a wider range of opportunities for personal and professional growth. You can invest in education, travel, or career advancement opportunities that support your goals.

EMERGENCY PREPAREDNESS:

Financial security ensures you are prepared for unexpected emergencies or setbacks, allowing you to maintain your focus on your long-term goals.

INCREASED CONFIDENCE:

Knowing you have financial stability can boost your confidence in pursuing challenging goals. You are more likely to believe in your ability to achieve what you set out to do.

STRATEGIC INVESTMENT:

Financial security allows you to strategically invest in assets or ventures that can contribute to your long-term goals, such as buying a home or starting a business.

LONG-TERM PLANNING:

Financial security enables you to engage in long-term planning with confidence. You can set and work toward goals that may take several years to achieve.

DEBT REDUCTION:

Financial security often includes the ability to pay off debts and loans. Reducing financial obligations frees up resources for goal-related activities.

PEACE OF MIND:

Financial security provides peace of mind. You can focus on your goals without constant worry about financial instability.

FOCUS ON PERSONAL GROWTH:

Financial security allows you to invest in personal growth and development, such as pursuing education, certifications, or personal enrichment activities.

RETIREMENT PLANNING:

A financially secure future often includes robust retirement planning. You can set retirement goals and work toward them with confidence.

REDUCED RISK AVERSION:

Financial security can reduce risk aversion, enabling you to take calculated risks that are necessary for achieving certain goals.

INCREASED GOAL COMMITMENT:

When you have financial security, you are more committed to your goals. You are less likely to be derailed by financial setbacks or unexpected expenses.

ASSET ACCUMULATION:

Financial security allows you to accumulate assets, such as investments or real estate, that can appreciate in value over time and contribute to your overall financial well-being.

GENERATIONAL IMPACT:

Financial security can extend to future generations. You can plan for your family's financial future and set goals that benefit your children or heirs.

PHILANTHROPIC ENDEAVORS:

Financial security may provide the means to engage in philanthropic activities or support causes that are important to you, allowing you to make a positive impact on society.

IMPROVED HEALTH AND WELL-BEING:

Financial security can lead to improved physical and mental well-being, as financial stress is a significant source of strain on both.

ENHANCED QUALITY OF LIFE:

Financial security contributes to an enhanced quality of life. You can enjoy a higher standard of living and access resources that enhance your overall well-being.

In summary, financial security is a fundamental component of successful goal setting. It provides the stability, confidence, and resources needed to pursue a wide range of goals effectively. With financial security, you have the freedom and flexibility to set and achieve both short-term and long-term objectives, leading to a more fulfilling and purpose-driven life.

IMPROVED RELATIONSHIPS

- Setting goals for personal or professional relationships can lead to better communication, understanding, and connection with others.

Improving relationships, whether they are personal, professional, or social, can have significant advantages when it comes to goal setting. Strong, positive relationships can provide valuable support, resources, and motivation to help you achieve your objectives. Here are the advantages of improving relationships in the context of goal setting:

SUPPORT AND ENCOURAGEMENT:

Improved relationships often come with a support system that can provide encouragement, motivation, and emotional support as you work toward your goals.

NETWORKING OPPORTUNITIES:

Building and strengthening relationships can expand your professional network, which can open doors to new opportunities, collaborations, and partnerships that support your goals.

RESOURCE SHARING:

Positive relationships can lead to resource sharing, including knowledge, skills, advice, and access to resources that are relevant to your goals.

ACCOUNTABILITY:

Trusted relationships can help hold you accountable for your goals. Sharing your goals with others can motivate you to stay on track and make consistent progress.

POSITIVE INFLUENCE:

Healthy relationships can have a positive influence on your mindset, attitude, and behavior, making it easier to stay focused, motivated, and optimistic about your goals.

CONFLICT RESOLUTION:

Improving relationships often involves developing conflict resolution skills. This can help you navigate disagreements and challenges more effectively, reducing potential obstacles to your goals.

COLLABORATIVE OPPORTUNITIES:

Positive relationships can lead to collaborative opportunities that allow you to work with others who share similar goals or complementary skills and resources.

FEEDBACK AND PERSPECTIVE:

Trusted relationships provide a source of feedback and a different perspective on your goals. This can help you refine your plans and make informed decisions.

MENTORSHIP AND GUIDANCE:

Building strong relationships can lead to mentorship or guidance from experienced individuals who can offer valuable insights and advice related to your goals.

ENHANCED COMMUNICATION:

Improving relationships often involves honing your communication skills. Effective communication is essential for conveying your goals and seeking support and cooperation from others.

REDUCED STRESS:

Positive relationships can contribute to reduced stress levels, allowing you to focus your energy and attention on your goals rather than dealing with relationship-related tension or conflicts.

EMOTIONAL RESILIENCE:

Strong relationships can enhance your emotional resilience. You are better equipped to handle setbacks or failures when you have a support network to lean on.

INCREASED CONFIDENCE:

Positive relationships can boost your self-confidence, making you more self-assured in pursuing challenging goals.

DIVERSE PERSPECTIVES:

Building relationships with people from different backgrounds and experiences can provide you with diverse perspectives and ideas, which can be valuable for goal achievement.

ENHANCED TEAMWORK:

In a professional or collaborative context, improving relationships can lead to stronger teamwork and cooperation, which can significantly impact the success of shared goals.

IMPROVED INTERPERSONAL SKILLS:

The process of building and maintaining relationships can help you develop essential interpersonal skills, including empathy, active listening, and conflict resolution.

PERSONAL GROWTH:

Building positive relationships often involves personal growth and self-awareness, which can positively impact your overall development and goal-setting abilities.

SOCIAL SUPPORT:

Strong relationships can provide a broader social support system, which is essential for maintaining mental and emotional well-being while pursuing your goals.

Improving relationships can be a strategic approach to goal setting that offers numerous advantages. Strong relationships provide support, resources, motivation, and a positive environment that can facilitate goal achievement. By nurturing and enhancing your relationships, you can create a valuable network of allies and supporters who can help you succeed in your personal and professional pursuits.

In summary, goal setting is a powerful tool for personal and professional development. It provides direction, motivation, and a framework for achieving your desired outcomes and improving various aspects of your life. Whether your goals are related to career, health, relationships, or personal growth, the benefits of goal setting are numerous and can lead to a more fulfilling and successful life.

PART 5

TYPES OF GOALS:

SHORT TERM GOALS

- These are typically goals you want to achieve within a few days, weeks, or months.

- Short-term goals are typically objectives you aim to achieve in the near future, usually within days, weeks, or a few months.

- Examples: Completing a project by the end of the week, going to the gym three times a week for the next month, or saving a specific amount of money by the end of the quarter.

Short-term goals are specific, measurable, and achievable objectives that you aim to accomplish within a relatively brief time frame, typically within days, weeks, or months. These goals are an essential part of goal setting and can serve as building blocks toward achieving longer-term objectives. Here's all you need to know about short-term goals:

CHARACTERISTICS OF SHORT-TERM GOALS:

Specific:

Short-term goals are clearly defined and specific. They answer the questions of what, why, how, and when. They are not vague or open-ended.

Measurable:

Short-term goals are quantifiable and measurable. You can track your progress and determine when you've successfully achieved the goal.

Achievable:

Short-term goals are realistic and attainable within the given time frame. They should be challenging but not so difficult that they are impossible to reach.

Time-Bound:

Short-term goals have a specific time frame or deadline by which they should be accomplished. This adds a sense of urgency and helps with time management.

Relevant:

Short-term goals are relevant to your broader objectives. They should align with your long-term goals or overall life plan.

EXAMPLES OF SHORT-TERM GOALS:

Professional Goals:

- Complete a specific project at work within the next month.
- Attend a professional development seminar within the next quarter.
- Secure a new job or promotion within six months.

Academic Goals:

- Achieve a certain grade point average (GPA) for the current semester.
- Finish a specific course or assignment by a set deadline.
- Obtain a specific certification or degree within a defined time frame.

Financial Goals:

- Save a certain amount of money in the next three months.
- Pay off a specific debt within the next year.
- Create a monthly budget and stick to it for the next six months.

Health and Fitness Goals:

- Lose a certain amount of weight within three months.

- Exercise a certain number of days per week for the next two months.

- Cut out a specific unhealthy habit (e.g., smoking, excessive sugar consumption) within one month.

Personal Development Goals:

- Read a certain number of books or complete a specific online course within the next few months.

- Develop a new skill or hobby within three months.

- Improve time management by implementing a new system in the next two weeks.

ADVANTAGES OF SHORT-TERM GOALS:

Immediate Progress:

Short-term goals allow you to experience a sense of achievement quickly, boosting motivation and confidence.

Focus:

They help you concentrate on specific tasks and priorities, reducing distractions.

Adaptability:

Short-term goals can be adjusted or modified more easily than long-term goals to accommodate changing circumstances.

Measurement:

Progress toward short-term goals is easily measured, providing feedback and opportunities for course correction.

Momentum:

Achieving short-term goals can build momentum and create a sense of progress toward larger, long-term goals.

Task Breakdown:

They enable you to break down complex, long-term goals into manageable, actionable steps.

Motivation:

Success with short-term goals can boost motivation and commitment to tackling more significant, longer-term objectives.

Learning:

Short-term goals offer opportunities to learn from both successes and failures, improving your skills and strategies.

Incorporating short-term goals into your overall goal-setting strategy is a practical way to make steady progress toward your larger aspirations. They provide structure, focus, and a sense of accomplishment, making them an integral part of achieving your desired outcomes.

LONG TERM GOALS

- These are goals set for the distant future, often spanning several years or even a lifetime.

- Long-term goals are aspirations that span an extended period, often several years or even a lifetime.

- Examples: Obtaining a master's degree, starting your own business, achieving financial independence, or retiring comfortably.

Long-term goals are ambitious, broad objectives that you aim to achieve over an extended period, often spanning several years or even decades. These goals are an integral part of goal setting and are typically connected to your broader life vision and purpose. Here's all you need to know about long-term goals:

CHARACTERISTICS OF LONG-TERM GOALS:

Ambitious:

Long-term goals are substantial and may require significant effort, dedication, and persistence to accomplish.

Future-Oriented:

They are focused on your vision of the future and the kind of life or career you want to create for yourself in the long run.

Broad and Comprehensive:

Long-term goals often encompass multiple aspects of your life, such as career, education, finances, health, relationships, and personal development.

Less Specific:

Unlike short-term goals, long-term goals are typically less detailed and specific because they cover a more extended time frame.

Measurable:

Although they may not have specific metrics, long-term goals should be measurable to some extent, allowing you to track progress over time.

Realistic:

While long-term goals can be ambitious, they should still be realistic and attainable within the context of your abilities, resources, and circumstances.

Time-Bound:

Long-term goals often lack specific deadlines but should have a general time frame in which you aim to achieve them.

Aligned with Values:

They should align with your core values, vision for your life, and personal priorities.

EXAMPLES OF LONG-TERM GOALS:

Career Goals:

- Attain a specific leadership position within your organization.
- Establish and run your own successful business.
- Transition into a new career field or industry.

Educational Goals:

- Obtain an advanced degree, such as a master's or doctorate.
- Pursue lifelong learning by continuously acquiring new skills and knowledge.

- Become a recognized expert in a particular field.

Financial Goals:

- Achieve financial independence and retire comfortably.

- Save a substantial amount for a major life event, such as buying a home or funding a child's education.

- Build significant wealth and leave a financial legacy.

Health and Wellness Goals:

- Maintain a high level of physical fitness and overall health throughout your life.

- Achieve and maintain a healthy body weight and lifestyle.

- Incorporate sustainable wellness practices into your daily routine.

Relationship Goals:

- Build and maintain strong, lasting relationships with family and friends.

- Find a life partner and create a loving, fulfilling relationship.

- Foster positive connections within your community or social circles.

Personal Development Goals:

- Develop a strong sense of self-awareness and emotional intelligence.

- Cultivate resilience and a growth mindset.

- Continuously work on improving personal skills, such as communication or leadership.

ADVANTAGES OF LONG-TERM GOALS:

Purpose and Direction:

Long-term goals provide a sense of purpose and direction in life, helping you navigate decisions and prioritize your actions.

Motivation:

They serve as a powerful source of motivation and inspiration, keeping you focused on your vision for the future.

Big-Picture Thinking:

Long-term goals encourage you to think beyond immediate concerns and make choices that align with your long-range objectives.

Planning and Strategy:

They necessitate careful planning and strategic thinking, helping you create a roadmap to achieve your vision.

Commitment:

Long-term goals require sustained commitment and dedication, fostering discipline and resilience.

Life Satisfaction:

Achieving long-term goals contributes to overall life satisfaction, fulfillment, and a sense of accomplishment.

Legacy and Impact:

Long-term goals often involve leaving a lasting legacy or making a significant impact on your community, industry, or the world.

Adaptability:

They can be adapted and adjusted over time to account for changing circumstances, priorities, and opportunities.

Milestone Measurement:

Long-term goals provide milestones for evaluating progress and celebrating achievements along the way.

Continuous Growth:

Pursuing long-term goals fosters personal growth, learning, and development over the course of your journey.

Self-Reflection:

They encourage self-reflection and self-discovery as you work toward your aspirations.

In summary, long-term goals are essential for providing direction, motivation, and purpose in your life. They encompass a wide range of areas, from career and education to health, relationships, and personal development. By setting and pursuing long-term goals, you can create a roadmap for your future and make significant strides toward realizing your desired life outcomes.

OUTCOME GOALS

- These specify the desired end result, such as winning a competition or achieving a specific career position.

- Outcome goals focus on a specific result or end state that you want to attain.

- Examples: Winning a sports championship, earning a promotion, losing a certain amount of weight, or publishing a book

Outcome goals, also known as results-based goals, are specific objectives that focus on the end result or outcome you want to achieve. These goals are often the final destination in your goal-setting journey and represent the ultimate achievement you're aiming for. Outcome goals are important because they provide a clear target to work toward and can help you stay motivated and focused on your desired outcome. Here's all you need to know about outcome goals:

CHARACTERISTICS OF OUTCOME GOALS:

Specific Result:

Outcome goals are defined by a specific, measurable result or achievement that you want to reach. They answer the question, "What do I want to accomplish?"

End Point:

These goals represent the endpoint or final destination of your efforts. They are typically set for the long term and may take months or even years to achieve.

External Focus:

Outcome goals are often influenced by external factors and may be somewhat beyond your direct control. They are the result of your actions and decisions but can also be influenced by other variables.

Motivational:

The prospect of achieving an outcome goal can be highly motivating. It provides a clear sense of purpose and a compelling reason to stay committed to your actions.

Measurable:

Outcome goals should be measurable to track progress and determine when they have been achieved. Measuring progress helps you stay on course and make adjustments as needed.

Challenging:

Outcome goals are typically challenging and may require significant effort and commitment to accomplish. They often stretch your abilities and push you beyond your comfort zone.

Long-Term:

These goals are usually set for the long term and are not meant to be achieved quickly. They require sustained effort and dedication over an extended period.

EXAMPLES OF OUTCOME GOALS:

Sports and Athletics:

- Win a championship or tournament in your sport.
- Qualify for the Olympic Games or a major international competition.
- Achieve a specific ranking or record in your sport

Business and Career:

- Become the CEO or president of a company.
- Reach a certain level of annual income or revenue.

- Expand your business to a certain number of locations or markets.

Education and Academics:

- Earn a Ph.D. or other advanced degree.
- Graduate with honors or a specific GPA.
- Become a recognized expert in a particular field.

Health and Fitness:

- Achieve a specific body weight or body composition.
- Complete a marathon or ultramarathon race.
- Attain a high level of proficiency in a particular sport or physical skill.

Personal Development:

- Write and publish a book or become a best-selling author.
- Achieve a specific level of proficiency in a musical instrument or art form.
- Make a significant positive impact on a cause or social issue.

ADVANTAGES OF OUTCOME GOALS:

Clarity and Focus:

Outcome goals provide clear direction and focus by defining the specific result you're aiming for.

Motivation:

They are highly motivating because they represent the ultimate achievement and reward for your efforts.

Measurable Progress:

Outcome goals can be broken down into smaller milestones, allowing you to measure progress along the way.

Long-Term Vision:

They contribute to your long-term vision and help you create a roadmap for your future.

Challenge and Growth:

Outcome goals often push you to grow, develop new skills, and overcome obstacles, fostering personal and professional growth.

Recognition and Achievement:

Achieving an outcome goal is often accompanied by recognition, accolades, and a sense of achievement.

Accountability:

Outcome goals provide a clear benchmark for accountability, helping you stay committed to your actions.

CONSIDERATIONS FOR OUTCOME GOALS:

Set SMART Subgoals:

Break down your outcome goals into smaller, specific, measurable, achievable, relevant, and time-bound (SMART) subgoals to make them more manageable.

Focus on Process Goals:

While outcome goals are important, it's equally crucial to set process goals that outline the actions and behaviors needed to achieve the desired outcome.

Adaptability:

Be prepared to adapt your approach if circumstances change or if you encounter unexpected challenges on your journey toward an outcome goal.

Celebrate Progress:

Celebrate your achievements and milestones along the way to maintain motivation and acknowledge your hard work.

In summary, outcome goals are the ultimate achievements you aim to reach in various aspects of your life. They provide clarity, motivation, and a long-term vision for your future. While outcome goals are essential, it's crucial to complement them with process goals and regularly evaluate your progress to ensure you stay on track.

PROCESS GOALS

- These focus on the actions, habits, and behaviors required to reach your outcome goals.

- Process goals emphasize the actions, behaviors, and steps you need to take to reach your desired outcome.

- Examples: Completing daily writing sessions, practicing a musical instrument for a specific amount of time each day, or consistently networking to enhance your career.

Process goals are a type of goal that focuses on the actions, behaviors, or processes you need to perform to achieve a desired outcome. These goals emphasize the journey or the steps you take rather than solely fixating on the end result. Here are the characteristics, advantages, and examples of process goals:

CHARACTERISTICS OF PROCESS GOAL

Action-Oriented:

Process goals are action-oriented. They define the specific actions, behaviors, or tasks you need to undertake to move toward your desired outcome.

Measurable:

Process goals are often measurable, allowing you to track your progress and know when you've successfully completed a particular action or behavior.

Controllable:

They focus on elements within your control. Unlike outcome goals, which can be influenced by external factors, process goals depend mainly on your efforts and actions.

Incremental:

Process goals break down larger objectives into smaller, manageable steps. This makes the overall goal less overwhelming and more achievable.

ADVANTAGES OF PROCESS GOALS:

Increased Focus:

Process goals keep you focused on the day-to-day or moment-to-moment tasks required to reach your ultimate objective.

Enhanced Motivation:

Regularly achieving process goals provides a sense of accomplishment and boosts motivation, keeping you engaged in the pursuit of your larger goals

Better Tracking:

Since process goals are measurable, they enable you to track your progress more effectively. This helps you make informed adjustments to your approach.

Resilience:

Focusing on the process can help you maintain a positive attitude, even in the face of setbacks or challenges. You're more likely to persevere because you value the journey itself

Continuous Improvement:

Process goals encourage a growth mindset by emphasizing improvement and development. You strive to do better with each step, leading to long-term progress.

EXAMPLES OF PROCESS GOALS:

Fitness Goal (Outcome Goal):

Run a marathon in under four hours.

- Process Goal:

☐ Complete a weekly training schedule that includes specific mileage targets, speed workouts, and cross-training activities.

Career Goal (Outcome Goal):

Secure a promotion to a management position.

- Process Goal:

  ☐ Attend leadership workshops or courses, take on additional responsibilities, and seek regular feedback from supervisors.

Academic Goal (Outcome Goal):

Graduate with honors.

- Process Goal:

  ☐ Allocate a set number of hours each day to study, complete all assignments on time, and seek help from professors when needed.

Weight Loss Goal (Outcome Goal):

Lose 20 pounds.

- Process Goal:

  ☐ Eat a balanced diet within a specific calorie range, exercise for a set number of minutes per day, and keep a food journal.

Relationship Goal (Outcome Goal):

Improve communication in a romantic relationship.

- Process Goal:

  ☐ Engage in active listening during daily conversations, attend couples' therapy sessions, and practice conflict resolution skills.

Financial Goal (Outcome Goal):

Save $10,000 for a vacation.

- Process Goal:

  ☐ Create a monthly budget, automate a portion of your salary for savings, and track expenses to stay within the budget.

Process goals are particularly effective in helping you stay motivated and maintain momentum throughout your journey. They provide clarity on what you need to do to reach your desired outcome and offer a sense of control over your progress. By incorporating process goals into your goal-setting approach, you can increase your chances of achieving your larger objectives.

GOALS CATEGORIZATION

Goals can be categorized into various types based on their characteristics and the areas of life they pertain to. Here are some common types of goals:

PERSONAL GOALS:

- Personal goals are related to self-improvement, personal development, and well-being.

- Examples: Learning a new language, improving communication skills, cultivating a positive mindset, or traveling to new destinations.

Personal goals are individualized objectives that you set for yourself to improve various aspects of your life, grow personally, or achieve specific outcomes that are meaningful to you. These goals are unique to your aspirations, values, and desires and can encompass a wide range of areas, from self-improvement and health to relationships and life experiences. Here's all you need to know about personal goals:

CHARACTERISTICS OF PERSONAL GOALS:

Individualized:

Personal goals are tailored to your personal values, interests, and priorities. They reflect what matters most to you.

Varied and Diverse:

Personal goals can cover a broad spectrum of areas, including health and fitness, education, career, relationships, hobbies, and personal development.

Flexible:

Unlike some other types of goals, personal goals are flexible and can change over time as your interests and priorities evolve.

Motivating:

Personal goals are highly motivating because they are inherently tied to your personal desires and passions.

Long-Term or Short-Term:

Personal goals can be either long-term or short-term, depending on the specific objectives you want to achieve.

Subjective Measurement:

These goals are often measured subjectively, based on your own feelings, satisfaction, and sense of accomplishment.

EXAMPLES OF PERSONAL GOALS:

Health and Fitness:

- Lose a specific amount of weight or achieve a target body composition.
- Run a marathon or complete a certain number of fitness classes.
- Adopt a healthier diet and lifestyle.

Personal Development:

- Develop better time management and organization skills.
- Enhance emotional intelligence and self-awareness.
- Improve public speaking or communication skills.

Relationships:

- Strengthen relationships with family members or friends.
- Find a life partner or improve an existing relationship.
- Build a more extensive social network.

Education and Learning:

- Pursue higher education, such as obtaining a degree or certification.

- Master a new language, skill, or art form.

- Read a specific number of books or explore a particular field of knowledge.

Career and Work:

- Attain a certain job position or level of responsibility.

- Increase income or financial stability.

- Launch your own business or pursue a specific career change.

Hobbies and Interests:

- Learn to play a musical instrument or excel in a hobby.

- Travel to specific destinations or have unique travel experiences.

- Engage in creative activities like painting, writing, or photography.

Personal Well-Being:

- Manage stress and improve mental health.

- Cultivate mindfulness and meditation practices.

- Achieve work-life balance and self-care.

ADVANTAGES OF PERSONAL GOALS:

Alignment with Values:

Personal goals align with your core values and desires, providing a sense of purpose and fulfillment.

Motivation:

They are inherently motivating because they reflect your interests and passions, driving you to take action.

Self-Improvement:

Personal goals contribute to your personal growth and development, fostering continuous learning and skill development.

Enhanced Satisfaction:

Achieving personal goals leads to increased satisfaction and a sense of accomplishment, contributing to overall well-being.

Customization:

You have complete control over the selection and prioritization of personal goals, making them tailored to your needs.

Empowerment:

Pursuing personal goals empowers you to take control of your life and create the future you desire.

Sense of Direction:

Personal goals provide a clear sense of direction and purpose, helping you navigate life's challenges.

CONSIDERATIONS FOR PERSONAL GOALS:

Prioritization:

It's important to prioritize personal goals based on what matters most to you at a given time in your life.

SMART Criteria:

Use the SMART criteria (Specific, Measurable, Achievable, Relevant, Time-bound) to set clear and actionable personal goals.

Balance:

Strive for a balance between various areas of personal growth and well-being, avoiding excessive focus on one area at the expense of others.

Adaptability:

Be open to adjusting personal goals as your circumstances, interests, and priorities change over time.

Accountability:

Share your personal goals with trusted individuals who can provide support, encouragement, and accountability.

In summary, personal goals are deeply individualized objectives that reflect your values, interests, and aspirations. They cover a wide array of areas and can have a significant impact on your personal growth, well-being, and life satisfaction. Setting and pursuing personal goals allows you to take charge of your life and work toward the outcomes that bring you the most fulfillment and happiness.

CAREER GOALS

- Career goals are oriented toward professional advancement, skill development, or achieving success in the workplace.
- Examples: Earning a job promotion, acquiring a new certification, increasing your salary, or launching a new project.

Career goals are specific objectives and aspirations related to your professional life and work. These goals help you outline a clear path for your career, guide your professional development, and provide direction for your future in the workplace. Setting and pursuing career goals is a key component of career planning and can lead to personal and professional fulfillment. Here's all you need to know about career goals:

CHARACTERISTICS OF CAREER GOALS:

Professional Focus:

Career goals are centered on your professional life, including your job, occupation, or career field.

Long-Term Vision:

They often encompass your long-term vision for your career, looking beyond immediate job responsibilities.

Specific and Measurable:

Career goals are specific and quantifiable, so you can track your progress and determine when you've achieved them.

Strategic:

They require careful planning, strategy, and action steps to reach desired career milestones.

Aligned with Values and Interests:

Career goals should align with your personal values, interests, skills, and passions to foster career satisfaction.

Adaptable:

While long-term, career goals may need to be adapted over time to reflect changes in your career aspirations or external factors.

Motivating:

Pursuing career goals can be highly motivating, driving you to excel and take ownership of your professional development.

EXAMPLES OF CAREER GOALS:

Advancement Goals:

- Obtain a specific job title, such as manager or director.
- Achieve a leadership position within your organization.
- Be promoted to a higher level in your career field.

Education and Skill Development:

- Earn a relevant degree, certification, or advanced training.
- Master a new skill or technology that is in demand in your industry.
- Expand your knowledge and expertise in a specific area.

Financial Goals:

- Increase your income or salary to a certain level.
- Achieve a specific savings or investment target.
- Eliminate financial debt related to your career or education

Networking and Professional Relationships:

- Expand your professional network within your industry or field.

- Establish mentorship relationships with experienced professionals.
- Enhance your visibility and reputation within your professional community.

Career Change or Transition:

- Successfully transition into a new career or industry.
- Pursue entrepreneurship or self-employment.
- Make a significant shift in your job role or specialization.

Work-Life Balance:

- Achieve a better balance between your work and personal life.
- Set boundaries to maintain a healthier work-life equilibrium.
- Pursue remote or flexible work options to accommodate personal needs.

ADVANTAGES OF CAREER GOALS:

Direction and Purpose:

Career goals provide direction and a sense of purpose in your professional life, helping you make informed decisions.

Motivation:

They serve as a source of motivation, inspiring you to take proactive steps to advance in your career.

Professional Growth:

Pursuing career goals encourages continuous learning, skill development, and personal growth.

Achievement:

Accomplishing career goals brings a sense of accomplishment and boosts confidence in your professional abilities.

Financial Stability:

Many career goals are associated with increased income, financial stability, and improved financial well-being.

Career Satisfaction:

Setting and achieving career goals can lead to greater job satisfaction and fulfillment.

Recognition:

Advancing in your career often comes with recognition, rewards, and new opportunities.

CONSIDERATIONS FOR CAREER GOALS:

Alignment with Values:

Ensure that your career goals align with your personal values and principles for a more fulfilling career.

Realistic Planning:

Set career goals that are attainable based on your skills, qualifications, and current circumstances.

Regular Evaluation:

Regularly assess and adjust your career goals to stay aligned with changing career aspirations or external factors.

Networking:

Building and maintaining professional relationships can significantly support your career goals.

Mentorship:

Seek guidance and mentorship from experienced professionals who can help you navigate your career path.

Work-Life Balance:

Consider the impact of your career goals on your work-life balance and overall well-being.

In summary, career goals are essential for guiding your professional journey, personal growth, and long-term success in your chosen field. They provide a roadmap for your career development, helping you stay focused, motivated, and proactive in achieving your professional aspirations.

L e s s o n   4 6

FINANCIAL GOALS

- Financial goals involve managing money, savings, investments, and achieving financial security or independence.

- Examples: Saving for retirement, paying off debt, buying a home, or creating an emergency fund.

Financial goals are specific objectives related to your financial well-being and financial management that you set to achieve greater financial stability, security, and prosperity. These goals help you plan, save, invest, and make informed financial decisions to improve your financial situation over time. Here's all you need to know about financial goals in goal setting:

CHARACTERISTICS OF FINANCIAL GOALS:

Specific and Measurable:

Financial goals are well-defined and quantifiable, making it clear when you've achieved them. They answer questions like "How much?" and "By when?"

Realistic and Achievable:

They are set based on your current financial situation and are attainable with careful planning and discipline.

Time-Bound:

Financial goals have a set deadline or time frame by which you aim to achieve them. This adds urgency and helps with planning.

Varied and Comprehensive:

Financial goals can cover a wide range of financial aspects, including savings, investments, debt management, retirement planning, and more.

Aligned with Values:

They should align with your financial values, priorities, and long-term financial vision.

EXAMPLES OF FINANCIAL GOALS:

Emergency Fund:

Save a specific amount, such as three to six months' worth of living expenses, in an emergency fund for unexpected financial needs.

Debt Reduction:

Pay off high-interest debt, such as credit card debt, within a certain time frame.

Savings Goals:

Save for specific purposes like a down payment on a home, a dream vacation, your children's education, or a major purchase.

Investment Goals:

Invest in assets like stocks, bonds, or real estate to achieve a target investment portfolio value by a certain age or milestone.

Retirement Planning:

Plan for retirement by setting a target retirement age, estimating retirement expenses, and determining how much you need to save for a comfortable retirement.

Budgeting and Expense Management:

Implement a budgeting system to track and manage your income and expenses effectively.

Income Growth:

Set goals for increasing your income through career advancement, side businesses, or investments.

Tax Planning:

Strategize to minimize tax liabilities and take advantage of tax-advantaged accounts and strategies.

ADVANTAGES OF FINANCIAL GOALS:

Financial Stability:

Financial goals help you build a stable financial foundation and protect against unexpected setbacks.

Increased Savings:

They encourage disciplined saving habits, which can lead to greater financial security and independence.

Wealth Accumulation:

Achieving financial goals can lead to wealth accumulation and the ability to invest in opportunities that align with your financial vision.

Debt Reduction:

Financial goals can help you reduce and ultimately eliminate high-interest debt, freeing up resources for other financial objectives.

Retirement Readiness:

Planning for retirement through financial goals ensures you have the financial means to enjoy your post-career years comfortably.

Improved Financial Knowledge:

Setting and pursuing financial goals often requires learning about personal finance, investment strategies, and tax planning.

Peace of Mind:

Achieving financial goals can reduce financial stress and provide peace of mind about your financial future.

Financial Independence:

Financial goals can lead to financial independence, allowing you to make choices based on your preferences rather than financial necessity.

CONSIDERATIONS FOR FINANCIAL GOALS:

Prioritization:

Determine which financial goals are most important to you and prioritize them based on your values and circumstances.

Financial Planning:

Develop a comprehensive financial plan to map out your goals, set strategies, and monitor your progress.

Regular Review:

Regularly review and update your financial goals to adapt to changing life circumstances, income levels, and financial priorities.

Professional Guidance:

Consider seeking advice from a financial advisor or planner to create a tailored financial plan.

Behavioral Factors:

Be aware of behavioral biases and emotional triggers that can affect your financial decisions, and develop strategies to overcome them.

In summary, financial goals play a vital role in achieving financial security, independence, and prosperity. They provide direction and purpose in managing your finances, encourage smart financial habits, and help you work toward your long-term financial vision. Setting and pursuing financial goals is a proactive step toward taking control of your financial future.

Lesson 47

EDUCATIONAL GOALS

- Educational goals pertain to learning and academic achievements, such as obtaining degrees, certifications, or specific knowledge and skills.

- Examples: Completing a bachelor's degree, attending professional development courses, or mastering a new programming language.

Educational goals are specific objectives related to your learning and academic achievements. These goals guide your educational journey and help you acquire knowledge, skills, and qualifications to advance your career, personal growth, or other life aspirations. Here's all you need to know about educational goals in goal setting:

CHARACTERISTICS OF EDUCATIONAL GOALS:

Specific and Measurable:

Educational goals are clear and quantifiable, defining the knowledge or qualifications you aim to acquire. They answer questions like "What degree?" or "What GPA?"

Time-Bound:

They have a set deadline or time frame by which you aim to achieve them, such as completing a degree within a specified number of years.

Realistic and Achievable:

Educational goals should be attainable based on your abilities, resources, and circumstances. They should stretch you but not be overly ambitious.

Aligned with Interests:

Educational goals are often connected to your interests, passions, and career aspirations, ensuring that your learning is meaningful to you.

Varied and Comprehensive:

These goals can encompass a wide range of educational pursuits, including formal degrees, certifications, skill development, and lifelong learning.

EXAMPLES OF EDUCATIONAL GOALS:

Academic Degrees:

- Earn a bachelor's, master's, or doctoral degree in a specific field of study.

- Achieve a particular grade point average (GPA) or class ranking.

- Complete a degree program within a specified number of years.

Certifications and Credentials:

- Obtain professional certifications or licenses related to your career or industry.

- Achieve proficiency in a specific software program, language, or skill.

- Earn a teaching credential or qualify for a specialized profession.

Language and Cultural Proficiency:

- Achieve fluency in a foreign language.

- Gain cultural competence and understanding through studying or traveling.

Career Development:

- Pursue advanced training or courses to enhance your career prospects.

- Attend workshops or seminars to stay up-to-date in your field.

- Pursue executive education or leadership development programs.

Personal Development:

- Expand your knowledge in areas of personal interest, such as history, art, or philosophy.

- Take courses in personal development, leadership, or communication skills.

ADVANTAGES OF EDUCATIONAL GOALS:

Skill and Knowledge Acquisition:

Educational goals enable you to acquire new skills, knowledge, and qualifications to enhance your personal and professional life.

Career Advancement:

Achieving educational goals can open up career opportunities, increase earning potential, and improve job prospects.

Personal Growth:

Pursuing education fosters personal growth, critical thinking, and intellectual curiosity.

Competitive Advantage:

Educational goals can provide a competitive edge in the job market by demonstrating your commitment to learning and professional development.

Networking:

Educational pursuits often involve interactions with instructors, classmates, and professionals, leading to valuable networking opportunities.

Adaptability:

Continuous learning through educational goals helps you adapt to changes in your field or industry.

Self-Esteem and Confidence:

Achieving educational goals boosts self-esteem and confidence in your abilities.

CONSIDERATIONS FOR EDUCATIONAL GOALS:

Clarity of Purpose:

Clearly define the purpose and relevance of your educational goals to your overall career and life aspirations.

Plan and Schedule:

Develop a plan for achieving your educational goals, including timelines and milestones.

Resource Allocation:

Consider the resources, including time, finances, and support, required to pursue your educational goals.

Flexibility:

Be adaptable and open to revising your educational goals as your interests and career objectives evolve.

Support and Mentorship:

Seek guidance and mentorship from educators, professionals, or advisors who can help you navigate your educational journey.

Balancing Priorities:

Ensure a balance between your educational goals and other life responsibilities, such as work and family.

In summary, educational goals are crucial for personal and professional development, as they guide your pursuit of knowledge, skills, and qualifications. They provide direction, motivation, and a sense of achievement as you work toward becoming a more informed and capable individual. Setting and achieving educational goals is a lifelong process that contributes to your growth and success.

L e s s o n   4 8

HEALTH AND FITNESS GOALS

Health and fitness goals focus on physical well-being, exercise, diet, and overall health improvement.

- Examples: Losing weight, running a marathon, maintaining a healthy diet, or building muscle mass.

Health and fitness goals are specific objectives related to improving your physical well-being and overall health. These goals help you prioritize your health, make positive lifestyle changes, and maintain or achieve a healthy body and mind. Here's all you need to know about health and fitness goals in goal setting:

CHARACTERISTICS OF HEALTH AND FITNESS GOALS:

Specific and Measurable:

Health and fitness goals are clear and quantifiable, outlining the specific outcomes or changes you want to achieve. They answer questions like "How much weight?" or "How many days per week?"

Realistic and Achievable:

Goals should be attainable based on your current health and fitness level. They should be challenging but not overly ambitious, considering your age, abilities, and health status.

Time-Bound:

Setting a deadline or timeframe for your goals adds urgency and helps with planning. For example, you might aim to achieve a specific fitness level within three months.

Wellness-Focused:

These goals are centered on overall wellness, which includes physical fitness, mental health, nutrition, and other aspects of well-being.

Lifestyle Integration:

Health and fitness goals often involve making sustainable lifestyle changes, such as adopting healthy eating habits, regular exercise routines, and stress management techniques.

EXAMPLES OF HEALTH AND FITNESS GOALS:

Weight Management:

- Lose a specific amount of weight.
- Maintain a healthy body weight within a certain range.
- Achieve a target body mass index (BMI).

Physical Fitness:

- Increase endurance by running a certain distance or for a specific duration.
- Achieve a specific number of push-ups, sit-ups, or pull-ups.
- Improve flexibility or balance through regular stretching or yoga.

Nutrition and Diet:

- Consume a balanced diet with a certain number of servings of fruits and vegetables daily.
- Reduce sugar, processed foods, or unhealthy fats in your diet.
- Follow a specific dietary plan, such as a low-carb or Mediterranean diet.

Mental Health and Stress Management:

- Practice mindfulness meditation or deep breathing exercises daily.

- Reduce stress by incorporating relaxation techniques or time management strategies into your routine.

- Improve sleep quality and establish a consistent sleep schedule.

Wellness Screenings:

- Schedule and complete regular health check-ups, screenings, and preventive care appointments.

- Track specific health metrics, such as blood pressure, cholesterol levels, or blood sugar levels, and aim for target values.

Lifestyle Changes:

- Quit smoking or reduce alcohol consumption.

- Establish a consistent exercise routine, such as going to the gym three times a week.

- Incorporate more physical activity into your daily life, such as walking or biking to work.

ADVANTAGES OF HEALTH AND FITNESS GOALS:

Improved Physical Health:

Achieving these goals can lead to improved physical health, including increased fitness, lower body fat, and better cardiovascular health.

Mental Well-Being:

Health and fitness goals often include stress reduction and mental health improvement, leading to reduced anxiety and depression.

Enhanced Quality of Life:

A healthy lifestyle can improve overall well-being, energy levels, and daily functioning.

Disease Prevention:

Setting and achieving health goals can help prevent or manage chronic health conditions, such as diabetes, hypertension, and heart disease.

Longevity:

A healthy lifestyle is associated with a longer life expectancy and a higher quality of life in later years.

Motivation and Discipline:

Pursuing health and fitness goals requires motivation and discipline, which can spill over into other areas of your life.

CONSIDERATIONS FOR HEALTH AND FITNESS GOALS:

Consultation with Professionals:

Before starting a new exercise or dietary plan, consider consulting with a healthcare provider, nutritionist, or fitness expert.

Gradual Progress:

Be patient and acknowledge that progress may be gradual. Avoid crash diets or intense workout routines that are unsustainable.

Balanced Approach:

Aim for a balanced approach that encompasses physical fitness, nutrition, mental health, and stress management.

Support System:

Seek support from friends, family, or a fitness community to help you stay accountable and motivated.

Regular Monitoring:

Track your progress using methods like fitness journals, smartphone apps, or wearable fitness trackers.

Adaptability:

Be open to modifying your goals as your circumstances, health status, or fitness level changes.

In summary, health and fitness goals are essential for maintaining or improving your overall well-being. They provide direction and motivation for adopting healthier lifestyle habits, making positive changes in your physical and mental health, and reducing the risk of chronic diseases. Prioritizing these goals can lead to a happier, healthier, and more fulfilling life.

RELATIONSHIP GOALS

- Relationship goals involve improving or nurturing various types of relationships, including family, friendships, and romantic partnerships.

- Examples: Strengthening communication with a spouse, spending more quality time with children, or making new friends.

Relationship goals are specific objectives that individuals or couples set to improve, strengthen, or enhance their interpersonal relationships with others. These goals help promote healthy and fulfilling relationships with partners, family members, friends, and colleagues. Here's all you need to know about relationship goals in goal setting:

CHARACTERISTICS OF RELATIONSHIP GOALS:

Specific and Measurable:

Relationship goals are clear and quantifiable, defining the specific improvements or changes you want to see in your interactions or connections with others.

Mutual Focus:

In many cases, relationship goals involve mutual efforts, meaning both parties are actively working together to achieve the goal.

Realistic and Achievable:

Goals should be attainable, taking into account the dynamics and circumstances of the relationship. Unrealistic goals can lead to frustration.

Communication-Centered:

Effective communication is often a key component of relationship goals. This includes open and honest dialogue, active listening, and empathy.

Emotional Well-Being:

Relationship goals may aim to improve emotional well-being, resolve conflicts, enhance trust, or strengthen bonds.

EXAMPLES OF RELATIONSHIP GOALS:

Communication Improvement:

- Practice active listening during conversations.
- Schedule regular check-ins or "date nights" to foster communication in a romantic relationship.
- Learn and practice conflict resolution skills.

Trust Building:

- Share vulnerabilities and build trust by confiding in each other.
- Keep promises and be reliable to strengthen trust.
- Encourage open and honest discussions about feelings and concerns.

Quality Time:

- Spend more quality time together by participating in shared activities or hobbies.
- Create a technology-free zone during dinner or special moments to focus on each other.

Conflict Resolution:

- Develop strategies for resolving conflicts constructively, such as using "I" statements.
- Seek mediation or counseling if conflicts persist and negatively impact the relationship.

Supportive and Positive Interactions:

- Give compliments and express appreciation regularly.
- Be emotionally supportive during challenging times.
- Show affection through physical touch, hugs, or other gestures.

Family Relationship Goals:

- Strengthen relationships with family members by initiating regular family gatherings or discussions.
- Set boundaries and address any longstanding issues within the family.

Friendship Goals:

- Reconnect with old friends or make new friends by joining social clubs or organizations.
- Practice active listening and empathy when interacting with friends.

ADVANTAGES OF RELATIONSHIP GOALS:

Improved Communication:

Relationship goals promote better communication, leading to deeper understanding and connection.

Strengthened Bonds:

Achieving relationship goals can strengthen bonds and enhance trust and intimacy in relationships.

Conflict Resolution:

Goals centered on conflict resolution help manage disagreements constructively, reducing stress and tension.

Emotional Well-Being:

A focus on emotional well-being can lead to happier and more fulfilling relationships.

Healthy Boundaries:

Relationship goals often include setting and respecting healthy boundaries, which is essential for maintaining a balanced and respectful dynamic.

Mutual Growth:

Pursuing relationship goals can lead to mutual personal growth and a stronger partnership.

Long-Term Relationship Satisfaction:

Achieving relationship goals can contribute to long-term satisfaction and happiness in relationships.

CONSIDERATIONS FOR RELATIONSHIP GOALS:

Mutual Agreement:

Ensure that both parties involved in the relationship are on the same page and agree to work toward the goals.

Realistic Expectations:

Set realistic and achievable goals that take into account the unique dynamics of the relationship.

Communication:

Effective communication is crucial when discussing and working on relationship goals. Be open, honest, and willing to listen.

Evaluation and Adaptation:

Periodically evaluate the progress of your relationship goals and be open to adapting them based on changing circumstances.

Professional Help:

In some cases, seeking the assistance of a relationship counselor or therapist can be beneficial for achieving relationship goals, especially if there are significant challenges or conflicts.

In summary, relationship goals are essential for nurturing and maintaining healthy, fulfilling relationships with partners, family members, friends, and colleagues. They provide direction, promote effective communication, and help resolve conflicts, ultimately leading to stronger and more satisfying connections with others.

SOCIAL AND COMMUNITY GOALS

Social and community goals center on contributing to society, community involvement, and making a positive impact on the world.

- Examples: Volunteering for a charitable organization, advocating for a social cause, or participating in community cleanup efforts.

Social and community goals are objectives that individuals set to make a positive impact on their communities or society as a whole. These goals typically focus on contributing to the well-being of others, fostering positive social change, and building stronger, more inclusive communities. Here are the characteristics, advantages, and examples of social and community goals:

CHARACTERISTICS OF SOCIAL AND COMMUNITY GOALS:

Community-Centered:

These goals are centered around improving the welfare of a community, whether it's a local neighborhood, a city, a region, or even a global community.

Altruistic:

Social and community goals are often altruistic in nature, driven by a desire to help others and make a positive difference in society.

Collaborative:

Achieving social and community goals often requires collaboration with others, such as community organizations, nonprofits, or volunteers.

Impactful:

These goals aim to have a meaningful and lasting impact on individuals, groups, or society as a whole.

Sustainability:

Social and community goals often incorporate sustainability principles, promoting long-term solutions and responsible resource use.

ADVANTAGES OF SOCIAL AND COMMUNITY GOALS:

Sense of Purpose:

Pursuing these goals can provide a strong sense of purpose and fulfillment by contributing to the well-being of others.

Community Building:

Working toward common social and community goals can foster a sense of belonging and cohesion within a community or group.

Personal Growth:

Engagement in social and community activities can lead to personal growth, improved empathy, and a broader perspective on social issues.

Positive Impact:

Achieving social and community goals can bring about positive changes in society, addressing pressing issues and making life better for many.

Networking and Relationships:

Involvement in community initiatives can help individuals build valuable relationships and expand their network.

EXAMPLES OF SOCIAL AND COMMUNITY GOALS:

Environmental Sustainability:

Organize and participate in community clean-up events to improve the local environment and raise awareness about sustainability.

Youth Education:

Volunteer as a mentor or tutor to support underprivileged youth in their academic and personal development.

Homelessness Reduction:

Work with a local shelter or nonprofit organization to provide food, shelter, and resources to homeless individuals in your community.

Health and Wellness:

Create a community wellness program that promotes physical and mental health through activities like exercise classes, workshops, and support groups.

Social Justice:

Advocate for social justice by participating in rallies, raising awareness about important issues, and supporting organizations focused on human rights and equality.

Community Revitalization:

Collaborate with others to revitalize a neglected neighborhood by renovating public spaces, planting gardens, and improving infrastructure.

CONSIDERATIONS WHEN PURSUING SOCIAL AND COMMUNITY GOALS:

Community Needs:

Identify the specific needs and priorities of your community or the group you aim to support.

Sustainability:

Ensure that your goals and actions contribute to sustainable and long-lasting improvements, rather than short-term fixes.

Collaboration:

Seek opportunities for collaboration with local organizations, community leaders, and volunteers who share your goals.

Measuring Impact:

Establish ways to measure the impact of your efforts to track progress and make necessary adjustments.

Advocacy and Education:

In addition to direct actions, consider the importance of raising awareness and advocating for policy changes that align with your goals.

Diversity and Inclusion:

Promote diversity and inclusion in your efforts to ensure that everyone in the community benefits from your initiatives.

Social and community goals are essential for creating positive change and improving the well-being of society. They provide individuals with opportunities to give back, connect with others, and make a lasting impact on their communities and the world at large.

TRAVEL AND ADVENTURE GOALS

- These goals revolve around exploring new places, experiencing adventures, and broadening your horizons through travel.

- Examples: Visiting specific countries or landmarks, hiking a famous trail, or embarking on a cross-country road trip.

Travel and adventure goals are objectives that revolve around exploring new places, experiencing different cultures, and engaging in thrilling or challenging activities. These goals are often driven by a desire for adventure, personal growth, and the enrichment of one's life through travel experiences. Here are the characteristics, advantages, and examples of travel and adventure goals:

CHARACTERISTICS OF TRAVEL AND ADVENTURE GOALS:

Exploration:

These goals involve exploring new destinations, whether they are local or global, and discovering unique experiences.

Adventure:

Travel and adventure goals often include adventurous activities such as hiking, scuba diving, skydiving, or exploring remote and off-the-beaten-path locations.

Cultural Engagement:

Travelers aim to immerse themselves in different cultures, interact with locals, and learn about the history, traditions, and customs of the places they visit.

Personal Enrichment:

These goals are focused on personal growth, self-discovery, and broadening one's horizons through travel experiences.

Memories and Stories:

Travel and adventure goals often result in the creation of lasting memories and stories to share with others.

ADVANTAGES OF TRAVEL AND ADVENTURE GOALS:

Personal Growth:

Travel and adventure goals can lead to personal growth by pushing individuals out of their comfort zones, promoting resilience, and expanding their worldview.

Cultural Awareness:

Exploring different cultures and meeting people from diverse backgrounds can foster greater cultural awareness and tolerance.

Stress Reduction:

Traveling and embarking on adventures can serve as a break from daily routines, reduce stress, and rejuvenate the mind and body.

Creativity and Inspiration:

New experiences can spark creativity, inspire fresh ideas, and encourage self-reflection.

Bonding and Relationships:

Traveling with loved ones or making new friends during adventures can strengthen relationships and create lasting bonds.

EXAMPLES OF TRAVEL AND ADVENTURE GOALS:

Backpacking Adventure:

Embark on a backpacking journey through multiple countries, experiencing different cultures and landscapes.

Hiking Expeditions:

Set a goal to complete a specific number of challenging hikes or trekking routes within a certain timeframe.

Cultural Immersion:

Learn a new language and spend a year living in a foreign country to fully immerse yourself in the culture.

Adventure Sports:

Master a particular adventure sport, such as rock climbing, surfing, or snowboarding, and challenge yourself with advanced courses or competitions.

Solo Travel:

Set a goal to explore a certain number of destinations independently to build self-confidence and self-reliance.

Exploration of Natural Wonders:

Visit iconic natural wonders like the Grand Canyon, Machu Picchu, or the Great Barrier Reef.

CONSIDERATIONS WHEN PURSUING TRAVEL AND ADVENTURE GOALS:

Safety:

Prioritize safety by researching destinations, adhering to local regulations, and taking necessary precautions during adventurous activities.

Sustainability:

Practice responsible tourism by minimizing your environmental impact and respecting local communities and ecosystems.

Budgeting:

Plan your travel and adventure goals within a realistic budget, considering costs for transportation, accommodation, activities, and emergencies.

Health and Fitness:

Ensure that you are physically prepared for adventure activities and consider necessary training or preparation.

Cultural Sensitivity:

Respect local customs, traditions, and etiquette when interacting with people from different cultures.

Travel and adventure goals provide opportunities for enriching experiences, personal development, and memorable adventures. They allow individuals to step outside their comfort zones, create lasting memories, and gain a deeper appreciation for the diversity of the world.

CREATIVITY AND HOBBY GOALS

- Creativity and hobby goals involve pursuing artistic or recreational interests, hobbies, or creative outlets.

- Examples: Writing a novel, learning to paint, mastering a musical instrument, or starting a photography project.

Creativity and hobby goals are personal objectives that revolve around exploring, developing, and mastering creative pursuits and hobbies. These goals are typically driven by a passion for artistic expression, self-improvement, and the pursuit of enjoyment and personal satisfaction. Here are the characteristics, advantages, and examples of creativity and hobby goals:

CHARACTERISTICS OF CREATIVITY AND HOBBY GOALS:

Personal Expression:

These goals emphasize personal expression and the freedom to create, explore, or engage in activities that bring joy and fulfillment.

Skill Development:

Creativity and hobby goals often involve developing and honing specific skills, techniques, or talents related to a particular hobby or creative pursuit.

Passion-Driven:

Individuals set these goals based on their passions and interests, whether it's painting, writing, playing musical instruments, cooking, or any other hobby.

Enjoyment:

The primary motivation for these goals is the sheer enjoyment and satisfaction derived from engaging in creative activities or hobbies.

Personal Growth:

Pursuing creativity and hobby goals can lead to personal growth, increased self-esteem, and a sense of accomplishment.

ADVANTAGES OF CREATIVITY AND HOBBY GOALS:

Stress Relief:

Engaging in creative activities and hobbies can serve as a stress-relief outlet, allowing individuals to unwind and relax.

Self-Expression:

Creative pursuits provide a means for self-expression and the exploration of personal thoughts, emotions, and ideas.

Sense of Achievement:

Accomplishing goals in creative and hobby areas can boost self-esteem and provide a sense of achievement.

Enhanced Skills:

These goals encourage skill development and mastery, which can lead to improved competence and self-confidence.

Positive Mental Health:

Creative activities and hobbies contribute to positive mental health, fostering a sense of purpose, joy, and well-being.

EXAMPLES OF CREATIVITY AND HOBBY GOALS:

Artistic Mastery:

- Become proficient in a specific art form, such as painting, sculpture, or photography, by creating a certain number of works or completing advanced courses.

Writing Goals:

- Set objectives to write a novel, publish a collection of poems, or complete a series of short stories within a defined timeframe.

Musical Achievement:

- Learn to play a musical instrument, compose original music, or perform in a local band or ensemble.

Cooking and Culinary Goals:

- Develop culinary skills by mastering a particular cuisine, achieving proficiency in baking, or creating a signature dish.

Gardening and Horticulture:

- Set goals to cultivate a beautiful garden, achieve a successful harvest, or grow specific plant varieties.

Crafting and DIY Projects:

- Complete a series of DIY home improvement projects, create handmade gifts for family and friends, or master a specific crafting technique.

CONSIDERATIONS WHEN PURSUING CREATIVITY AND HOBBY GOALS:

Time Management:

- Allocate dedicated time for pursuing your creative activities and hobbies to ensure consistent progress.

Resources:

- Consider the availability of resources, materials, or equipment needed to pursue your chosen hobby or creative pursuit.

Learning Opportunities:

- Seek out workshops, classes, or online courses to enhance your skills and knowledge in your chosen area of interest.

Inspiration and Creativity:

- Explore new sources of inspiration, collaborate with others, and experiment with different techniques to keep your creativity flowing.

Balance:

- Strike a balance between pursuing your creative passions and other life commitments to prevent burnout and maintain well-roundedness.

Creativity and hobby goals provide an avenue for self-expression, personal growth, and enjoyment. They encourage individuals to explore their interests and passions, fostering a sense of accomplishment and well-being.

SPIRITUAL AND MINDFULNESS GOALS:

- These goals focus on spiritual growth, meditation, mindfulness practices, and achieving inner peace.

- Examples: Practicing daily meditation, attending religious or spiritual gatherings, or deepening your spiritual connection.

Creativity and hobby goals are objectives individuals set to explore, develop, or enhance their creative talents and pursue hobbies or interests that bring them joy and satisfaction. These goals focus on nurturing one's artistic, creative, or recreational pursuits, whether for personal enjoyment or with the intention of achieving a specific level of proficiency or accomplishment. Here's all you need to know about creativity and hobby goals in goal setting:

CHARACTERISTICS OF CREATIVITY AND HOBBY GOALS:

Passion-Driven:

These goals are often rooted in personal passions and interests, reflecting what individuals truly enjoy and are enthusiastic about.

Specific and Measurable:

Creativity and hobby goals are clear and well-defined, outlining the specific creative projects or achievements individuals aspire to accomplish.

Artistic and Recreational:

They encompass a wide range of activities, from artistic pursuits like painting and writing to recreational hobbies like sports or gardening.

Personal Growth:

Creativity and hobby goals often promote personal growth, self-expression, and skill development in a particular area of interest.

Self-Directed:

These goals are self-directed, allowing individuals to set their own objectives and pace for creative exploration or hobby engagement.

EXAMPLES OF CREATIVITY AND HOBBY GOALS:

Artistic Pursuits:

- Create a specific number of paintings or drawings within a defined timeframe.
- Write a novel, poetry collection, or screenplay.
- Learn a musical instrument and aim to play a certain number of songs proficiently.

Crafting and DIY Projects:

- Complete a series of DIY home improvement or craft projects.
- Learn a new crafting technique, such as knitting, woodworking, or pottery.
- Establish an online store to sell handmade crafts.

Sports and Fitness Hobbies:

- Set personal fitness goals, such as running a certain distance or achieving a particular level of strength.
- Participate in a specific number of sports events or competitions.
- Master a new sport or athletic skill, such as surfing, rock climbing, or yoga.

Gardening and Horticulture:

- Create a flourishing garden with specific plants, flowers, or vegetables.

- Learn about sustainable gardening practices and implement them.

- Achieve a certain level of expertise in bonsai tree cultivation.

Photography and Videography:

- Complete a photography project, such as a themed photo series.

- Learn advanced photography or videography techniques.

- Create a portfolio of high-quality photographs or videos.

ADVANTAGES OF CREATIVITY AND HOBBY GOALS:

Personal Fulfillment:

Engaging in creative pursuits and hobbies can bring joy, satisfaction, and a sense of accomplishment.

Stress Reduction:

Creative activities and hobbies provide a healthy outlet for stress relief and relaxation.

Skill Development:

Pursuing these goals can lead to the development of new skills and competencies in a chosen area of interest.

Self-Expression:

Creativity and hobbies offer a means of self-expression and a platform for sharing one's unique perspective with the world.

- Social Interaction:

Some hobbies provide opportunities to connect with like-minded individuals, fostering social interaction and community building.

Enhanced Well-Being:

Engaging in creative or recreational activities has been linked to improved mental and emotional well-being.

CONSIDERATIONS FOR CREATIVITY AND HOBBY GOALS:

Balance:

Ensure that your creative and hobby goals complement your overall lifestyle and other responsibilities.

Enjoyment:

Prioritize enjoyment and passion in your pursuits rather than solely focusing on achieving specific outcomes.

Skill Progression:

If skill development is a goal, create a plan for continuous learning and practice.

Resources:

Consider the resources needed, such as materials, equipment, or training, to pursue your chosen hobby or creative endeavor.

Challenge Level:

Strike a balance between setting challenging goals and maintaining a sense of enjoyment and relaxation in your hobby.

Adaptability:

Be open to adjusting your goals as your interests evolve or new opportunities arise.

In summary, creativity and hobby goals allow individuals to nurture their passions, explore new interests, and experience personal growth and fulfillment through creative expression and recreational pursuits. These goals offer a balanced approach to life, promoting well-being, self-expression, and the pursuit of activities that bring joy and satisfaction.

Remember that individuals may have a combination of these goal types, and the goals you set should align with your values, aspirations, and current life circumstances. Additionally, setting a mix of short-term and long-term goals can help you maintain a balanced approach to personal and professional growth.

P A R T 6

SETTING GOALS IN DIFFERENT AREAS OF LIFE:

You can set goals in various areas, including:

- Personal Goals: Related to health, fitness, relationships, personal development, and hobbies.

- Career Goals: Aimed at advancing in your career, acquiring new skills, or starting a business.

- Financial Goals: Focus on saving, investing, reducing debt, or achieving financial independence.

- Academic Goals: Relate to your education and learning objectives.

- Social Goals: Concerned with building and maintaining relationships with family, friends, and colleagues.

TYPES OF GOALS

Setting goals in different areas of life allows you to have a well-rounded and balanced approach to personal development and fulfillment. Here are some key areas where you can set goals:

CAREER GOALS:

- Advance in your career by setting goals related to job promotions, salary increases, or skill development.
- Achieve specific milestones or positions in your chosen field.
- Enhance job satisfaction or work-life balance by setting career-related goals.

FINANCIAL GOALS:

- Save and invest money for various financial objectives.
- Pay off debts, such as student loans, credit card debt, or mortgages.
- Achieve financial independence or early retirement.

EDUCATION AND LEARNING GOALS:

- Pursue further education or obtain additional certifications.
- Master new skills or languages.
- Set goals for academic achievement and lifelong learning.

HEALTH AND FITNESS GOALS:

- Improve physical health by setting goals related to weight loss, muscle gain, or improved endurance.

- Develop healthy eating habits and nutrition goals.

- Set fitness goals like running a marathon, achieving a specific body fat percentage, or regular exercise routines.

PERSONAL DEVELOPMENT GOALS:

- Work on personal growth by setting goals for self-improvement.

- Enhance emotional intelligence, self-awareness, and mindfulness.

- Develop better communication or time management skills.

RELATIONSHIP GOALS:

- Build and nurture healthy relationships with family, friends, or romantic partners.

- Improve communication within your relationships.

- Set goals for quality time spent with loved ones.

SOCIAL AND COMMUNITY GOALS:

- Give back to your community by volunteering or participating in charitable activities.

- Advocate for social causes or join organizations that align with your values.

- Set goals for networking and expanding your social circle.

CREATIVE AND HOBBY GOALS:

- Pursue creative interests and hobbies, such as painting, writing, or playing a musical instrument.

- Set artistic or creative goals, like completing a novel or mastering a new skill.

TRAVEL AND ADVENTURE GOALS:

- Explore new places and cultures by setting travel goals.

- Go on adventures like hiking, camping, or backpacking trips.

- Visit specific landmarks or destinations on your bucket list.

SPIRITUAL AND MINDFULNESS GOALS:

- Deepen your spiritual practice or explore new spiritual beliefs.

- Set goals for daily meditation, yoga practice, or mindfulness routines.

- Achieve a sense of inner peace and balance.

ENVIRONMENTAL AND SUSTAINABILITY GOALS:

- Contribute to environmental conservation by setting goals for reducing waste, conserving resources, or adopting sustainable practices.

- Support environmental causes or engage in eco-friendly initiatives.

PARENTING AND FAMILY GOALS:

- Focus on raising happy and healthy children by setting parenting goals.

- Strengthen family bonds and create a positive home environment.

- Achieve work-life balance as a parent.

TRAVEL AND ADVENTURE GOALS:

- Explore new places and cultures by setting travel goals.

- Go on adventures like hiking, camping, or backpacking trips.

- Visit specific landmarks or destinations on your bucket list.

SOCIAL AND COMMUNITY GOALS:

- Give back to your community by volunteering or participating in charitable activities.

- Advocate for social causes or join organizations that align with your values.

- Set goals for networking and expanding your social circle.

ENVIRONMENTAL AND SUSTAINABILITY GOALS:

- Contribute to environmental conservation by setting goals for reducing waste, conserving resources, or adopting sustainable practices.

- Support environmental causes or engage in eco-friendly initiatives.

PARENTING AND FAMILY GOALS:

- Focus on raising happy and healthy children by setting parenting goals.

- Strengthen family bonds and create a positive home environment.

- Achieve work-life balance as a parent.

RETIREMENT AND LONG-TERM PLANNING GOALS:

- Plan for your retirement by setting financial and lifestyle goals.

- Ensure financial security and have a fulfilling retirement.

- Consider estate planning and leaving a legacy.

Setting goals in these diverse areas of life can help you lead a more balanced, fulfilling, and purposeful existence. It's essential to prioritize goals based on your current circumstances and values, ensuring that they align with your overall life vision.

GOAL SETTING PROCESS

IDENTIFY GOALS:

- Determine what you want to achieve and why it's important to you.

Identifying and setting goals is a critical part of personal development and achievement. The process of identifying goals involves several steps to ensure that your goals are clear, meaningful, and achievable. Here's a step-by-step guide to help you identify and set goals effectively:

1. Self-Reflection:

- Begin by reflecting on your values, passions, and interests. Consider what truly matters to you in different areas of your life, such as career, health, relationships, and personal growth.

2. Define Your Priorities:

- Determine your short-term and long-term priorities. What are the most important aspects of your life that you want to focus on and improve?

3. Brainstorm Goals:

- Create a list of potential goals that align with your values and priorities. Be open-minded and creative during this stage. Don't worry about feasibility at this point; just generate ideas.

4. Categorize Your Goals:

- Group your goals into different categories or areas of your life. Common categories include career, health, relationships, personal development, finance, and leisure.

5. Evaluate and Prioritize:

- Assess each goal based on its significance, feasibility, and alignment with your values. Prioritize your goals, focusing on the most important ones that you're most motivated to pursue.

6. Make Your Goals SMART:

- Refine your goals to make them Specific, Measurable, Achievable, Relevant, and Time-bound (SMART). This framework ensures that your goals are clear and actionable.

- Example of a SMART goal: "Lose 15 pounds within the next six months by exercising for 30 minutes daily and following a balanced diet."

7. Break Down Long-Term Goals:

If you have long-term goals, break them down into smaller, manageable milestones or sub-goals. This makes them less overwhelming and more achievable.

- For instance, if your long-term goal is to start a successful business, your sub-goals might include market research, business plan development, and securing funding.

8. Set a Timeline:

- Assign specific deadlines or timelines to each goal and sub-goal. Having a timeframe adds urgency and accountability.

9. Write Your Goals Down:

- Document your goals in a written format. This could be in a notebook, digital document, or a goal-setting app. Writing them down reinforces your commitment and helps you track progress.

10. Visualize Success:

- Imagine what success looks like for each goal. Visualization can boost motivation and clarify your objectives.

11. *Share Your Goals:*

- Consider sharing your goals with a trusted friend, family member, or mentor. Accountability and support from others can help you stay on track.

12. *Review and Adjust:*

- Regularly review your goals to track progress and make adjustments as needed. Life circumstances may change, requiring modifications to your goals.

13. *Stay Committed:*

- Stay committed to your goals by taking consistent action steps. Focus on the daily or weekly tasks that will bring you closer to your objectives.

14. *Celebrate Achievements:*

- Celebrate your successes, no matter how small. Acknowledging your achievements can boost motivation and maintain a positive attitude.

15. *Seek Support and Guidance:*

- If you encounter challenges or obstacles, don't hesitate to seek support or guidance from mentors, coaches, or professionals who can provide assistance and advice.

16. *Stay Flexible:*

- Be open to adjusting your goals if necessary. Sometimes, you may discover new interests or priorities that require you to pivot.

Remember that goal setting is an ongoing process. As you achieve goals, you can set new ones to continue your personal growth and development. Regularly revisit and refine your goals to ensure they align with your evolving values and aspirations.

MAKE THEM SMART:

- Refine your goals using the SMART criteria.

The SMART process is a framework for setting goals that are Specific, Measurable, Achievable, Relevant, and Time-bound. This approach ensures that your goals are clear, well-defined, and more likely to be achieved. Here's how to make your goals SMART:

1. Specific:

- Start by making your goal as specific and precise as possible. Clearly define what you want to achieve. Ask yourself:
  - ☐ What exactly do I want to accomplish?
  - ☐ Why is this goal important?
  - ☐ Who is involved?
  - ☐ Where will it happen?
  - ☐ What are the requirements and constraints?
- Example of a non-specific goal: "Get in shape."
- Example of a specific goal: "Lose 15 pounds by exercising for 30 minutes daily and following a balanced diet."

2. Measurable:

- A goal should be quantifiable, allowing you to track progress and determine when you've achieved it. Ask yourself:
  - ☐ How will I measure progress and success?
  - ☐ How much or how many?
  - ☐ What criteria will I use to know when the goal is achieved?
- Example of a non-measurable goal: "Improve my fitness."
- Example of a measurable goal: "Run a 5K race in under 25 minutes within six months."

3. Achievable:

- Ensure that your goal is realistic and attainable. It should be challenging but still within your reach. Consider your abilities, resources, and time available. Ask yourself:

    - ☐ Is this goal realistic for me right now?

    - ☐ Do I have the necessary skills and resources?

    - ☐ Can I commit the time and effort required?

- Example of an unachievable goal: "Win an Olympic gold medal in a sport I've never tried."

- Example of an achievable goal: "Complete a certification course in my field within the next year."

4. Relevant:

- Your goal should be relevant and aligned with your values, priorities, and long-term objectives. Ask yourself:

    - ☐ Does this goal align with my values and long-term vision?

    - ☐ Is it the right time to pursue this goal?

    - ☐ Will it have a positive impact on my life?

- Example of an irrelevant goal: "Learn to play the guitar when my true passion is painting."

- Example of a relevant goal: "Improve my public speaking skills to advance my career."

5. Time-bound:

- Set a specific timeframe or deadline for achieving your goal. This adds urgency and helps with planning. Ask yourself:

    - ☐ When do I want to achieve this goal?

    - ☐ Is there a deadline that makes sense?

    - ☐ What can I do today, this week, and this month to move toward the goal?

- Example of a goal without a timeframe: "Learn a new language."

- Example of a time-bound goal: "Achieve conversational fluency in Spanish within one year."

By following the SMART process, you'll transform your goals into actionable and well-structured objectives that are more likely to lead to success. Regularly reviewing and revising your SMART goals will help you stay on track and adapt to changing circumstances as you work toward your aspirations.

BREAK DOWN GOALS:

- Divide larger goals into smaller, more manageable steps.

Breaking down goals is a crucial step in goal setting, especially when you have larger or more complex objectives. Breaking them into smaller, manageable parts makes them less overwhelming and more achievable. Here's a process for breaking down your goals effectively:

1. Start with a Clear Goal:

- Begin with a well-defined and specific goal. Make sure it follows the SMART criteria (Specific, Measurable, Achievable, Relevant, and Time-bound).

2. Identify the Key Components:

- Analyze your main goal and identify the key components or sub-objectives necessary to achieve it. Think about what needs to happen to make your goal a reality.

3. Create Milestones:

- Divide your goal into smaller milestones or stages. These are significant checkpoints along the way that will help you measure your progress.

4. Determine Action Steps:

- Break down each milestone further into actionable steps or tasks. These are the specific actions you need to take to reach each milestone.

5. Prioritize and Sequence:

- Organize your action steps in a logical sequence or order. Some tasks may need to be completed before others can begin.

6. Set Deadlines:

- Assign deadlines to each milestone and action step. Be realistic about the time required for each task.

7. Allocate Resources:

- Determine what resources you'll need for each task, such as time, money, tools, or assistance from others.

8. Monitor and Adjust:

- Regularly monitor your progress toward each milestone and make adjustments as needed. If you encounter unexpected challenges or changes in circumstances, be prepared to adapt your plan.

9. Stay Accountable:

- Hold yourself accountable for completing each action step by its deadline. You can use tools like to-do lists, project management apps, or calendars to help you stay on track.

10. Celebrate Achievements:

- Celebrate your successes as you reach each milestone. Recognizing your progress can boost motivation and maintain a positive attitude.

EXAMPLE: BREAKDOWN OF A CAREER GOAL:

Main Goal: "Secure a promotion to a management position within my current company within the next two years."

Key Components:

- Enhance leadership skills.
- Demonstrate increased responsibility.

- Build a strong professional network.
- Showcase achievements and contributions.

Milestones:

- Complete a leadership training program.
- Successfully lead a cross-functional project.
- Attend industry conferences and networking events.
- Prepare and present a proposal for a new initiative.

Action Steps for Milestone 1 - Leadership Training:

- Research available leadership programs.
- Enroll in a relevant leadership course.
- Attend all sessions and complete assignments.
- Apply new leadership skills in the workplace.

Action Steps for Milestone 2 - Leading a Project:

- Identify a suitable project within the company.
- Propose to lead the project to your supervisor.
- Assemble a project team.
- Develop a project plan and timeline.
- Execute the project, managing tasks and team members effectively.
- Present the project results to senior management.

Action Steps for Milestone 3 - Networking:

- Research upcoming industry conferences and events.
- Register for selected events and make necessary travel arrangements.
- Attend conferences and actively engage with industry professionals.
- Follow up with contacts and connect on professional social networks.

Action Steps for Milestone 4 - Proposal Presentation:

- Identify a relevant initiative or improvement opportunity within your department.

- Research and analyze the initiative thoroughly.

- Develop a detailed proposal for implementation.

- Schedule a presentation to senior management.

- Deliver a persuasive and well-prepared presentation.

By following this process, you can effectively break down your goals into manageable steps, making them more attainable and less overwhelming. This approach also provides a clear roadmap for your journey toward achieving your objectives.

CREATE AN ACTION PLAN:

- Outline the specific actions and tasks needed to achieve each goal.

Creating an action plan is a critical step in goal setting that outlines the specific tasks, timelines, and resources required to achieve your goals. Here's a process for creating an action plan:

1. Define Your Goal:

- Start with a clear and specific goal that you want to achieve. Ensure it is aligned with your values and priorities.

2. Identify Key Objectives:

- Break down your goal into smaller, measurable objectives or milestones that will lead to its accomplishment. These objectives should be specific and achievable.

3. List Actionable Tasks:

- For each objective, identify the actionable tasks or steps you need to take. Be as specific as possible. Consider what, when, where, and how each task will be completed.

4. Prioritize Tasks:

- Determine the order in which you need to complete the tasks. Some tasks may be dependent on others and should be prioritized accordingly.

5. Set Deadlines:

- Assign deadlines to each task and objective. Be realistic about the time needed for each task, and consider how they fit within your overall timeline.

6. Allocate Resources:

- Identify the resources you'll need for each task, such as time, money, materials, or assistance from others. Ensure you have access to these resources.

7. Create a Timeline:

- Develop a timeline that visually represents when each task and objective will be completed. Use a calendar or project management tool to help you stay organized.

8. Establish Accountability:

- Determine who is responsible for each task and objective. If you are working with others, assign roles and responsibilities to ensure everyone knows their part.

9. Monitor and Track Progress:

- Regularly review your action plan to monitor progress. Check off completed tasks and update timelines as needed. If you encounter delays or obstacles, adjust your plan accordingly.

10. Stay Flexible:

- Be open to adapting your action plan if circumstances change or new opportunities arise. Flexibility is important for staying on track toward your goal.

11. Seek Support and Assistance:

- If necessary, reach out to mentors, advisors, or experts who can provide guidance and support for specific tasks or objectives.

12. Maintain Motivation:

- Stay motivated by periodically revisiting your goal and reminding yourself why it's important to you. Celebrate small achievements along the way.

13. Measure Progress:

- Develop specific metrics or indicators to measure your progress toward each objective. This will help you assess whether you are on track or need to make adjustments.

14. Review and Adjust:

- Periodically review your action plan to evaluate its effectiveness. If you encounter challenges or find that certain tasks are not contributing to your goal, be willing to revise your plan.

15. Stay Committed:

- Commit to following your action plan consistently. Consistent effort and dedication are key to achieving your goals.

16. Celebrate Achievements:

- Celebrate your successes as you complete tasks and reach objectives. Recognizing your achievements will reinforce your commitment to your goal.

17. Continuously Update and Refine:

- As you make progress and learn from your experiences, update and refine your action plan. Your goals and priorities may evolve over time, so your action plan should adapt accordingly.

By following this process, you'll create a comprehensive action plan that provides a clear roadmap for achieving your goals. Whether your goals are personal, professional, or related to any area of your life, an action plan helps you stay organized, motivated, and on track toward success.

SET DEADLINES:

- Assign deadlines to each step or milestone to keep yourself accountable.

Setting deadlines in goal setting is a crucial component of ensuring that your goals are actionable and achievable within a specific timeframe. Here's how to set deadlines effectively:

1. Understand the Importance of Deadlines:

- Deadlines create a sense of urgency and accountability. They help you stay focused, organized, and committed to your goals.

2. Make Your Goals SMART:

- Before setting deadlines, ensure that your goals are Specific, Measurable, Achievable, Relevant, and Time-bound (SMART). This framework ensures that your goals are well-defined.

3. Prioritize Your Goals:

- Determine which goals are your top priorities. You may have short-term and long-term goals, so it's essential to know which ones you want to tackle first.

4. Break Down Your Goals:

- Divide your larger goals into smaller, manageable tasks or milestones. Breaking them down makes it easier to set deadlines for each component.

5. Set Realistic Timeframes:

- Be realistic when setting deadlines. Consider the complexity of the goal, the resources available, and your other commitments. Avoid setting overly ambitious or unrealistic deadlines that may lead to frustration.

6. Use a Calendar or Planner:

- Utilize a digital calendar, physical planner, or goal-setting app to schedule your deadlines. Having a visual representation of your timeline can help you stay organized.

7. Assign Specific Dates:

- Assign specific dates to each task or milestone related to your goal. Specify when you plan to start and finish each component.

8. Consider Milestones:

- If your goal is a long-term one, consider setting intermediate milestones with their own deadlines. These milestones act as checkpoints and progress indicators.

9. Be Accountable:

- Hold yourself accountable for meeting your deadlines. If you're working with others on a shared goal, ensure that everyone is aware of and committed to the deadlines.

10. Build in Buffer Time:

- Allow some buffer time when setting deadlines to account for unexpected delays or obstacles. Life can be unpredictable, so it's helpful to have a bit of flexibility in your schedule.

11. Regularly Review and Adjust:

- Periodically review your progress and deadlines. If you find that you're falling behind or that circumstances have changed, adjust your deadlines accordingly.

12. Communicate Your Deadlines:

- If your goals involve collaboration with others, communicate your deadlines clearly and ensure that everyone is on the same page.

13. Stay Motivated:

- Use your deadlines as motivation. Knowing that you have a specific date to work toward can help you maintain focus and commitment.

14. Celebrate Achievements:

- Celebrate your successes as you meet each deadline. Recognizing your progress can boost motivation and morale.

15. Be Flexible When Necessary:

- While it's essential to stick to deadlines, be open to adjusting them if circumstances change or if you realize that a deadline was initially unrealistic.

16. Learn from Missed Deadlines:

- If you miss a deadline, use it as an opportunity to learn. Analyze what caused the delay and how you can better manage your time in the future.

Setting deadlines is a practical way to turn your goals into actionable plans. It keeps you accountable, organized, and motivated as you work toward achieving your aspirations. Whether your goals are related to career, personal development, health, or any other area of your life, effective deadline setting is a key component of successful goal attainment.

MONITOR PROGRESS:

- Regularly assess your progress and adjust your plan as needed.

Monitoring progress is a crucial aspect of goal setting because it helps you stay on track, make adjustments when needed, and maintain motivation. Here's a process for effectively monitoring your progress in goal setting:

1. Define Measurable Metrics:

Before you start working on your goals, establish specific metrics or indicators that will allow you to measure your progress objectively. These metrics should align with the Measurable aspect of SMART goals.

2. Create a Tracking System:

Choose a tracking system that works for you. It could be a digital tool, a physical journal, a spreadsheet, or a goal-setting app. Ensure that it's easy to use and access.

3. Set Milestones and Checkpoints:

Break down your goals into smaller milestones or checkpoints. These are specific points in your timeline where you can evaluate your progress. Assign deadlines to these milestones.

4. Regularly Review Your Goals:

Schedule regular times to review your goals and assess your progress. This could be daily, weekly, or monthly, depending on the nature of your goals.

5. Compare Actual vs. Planned Progress:

During your reviews, compare your actual progress to what you had planned. Did you complete the tasks or reach the milestones you had set for that period?

6. Analyze Achievements and Challenges:

Celebrate your achievements and acknowledge your successes, no matter how small. Also, identify any challenges, setbacks, or obstacles you encountered

7. Adjust and Adapt:

If you're falling behind on your timeline or facing unexpected obstacles, be prepared to adjust your approach. Adapt your action plan or deadlines as necessary to get back on track.

8. Seek Feedback and Support:

If you're working on goals as part of a team or with a mentor, seek feedback and support during your progress reviews. Others can provide valuable insights and encouragement.

9. Stay Accountable:

Hold yourself accountable for the goals you've set. If you have an accountability partner, share your progress with them regularly.

10. Reflect on Your Efforts:

Reflect on your efforts and the strategies you've used. Are they effective? Are there areas where you could improve your approach?

11. Stay Motivated:

Keep your motivation high by reminding yourself of the reasons you set these goals in the first place. Visualize your desired outcomes and the benefits of achieving them.

12. Adjust Timeframes When Necessary:

If you realize that your initial timelines were too ambitious or too lenient, adjust them accordingly to ensure they remain realistic.

13. Learn from Mistakes and Failures:

If you encounter setbacks or failures, view them as opportunities for growth and learning. Analyze what went wrong and how you can avoid similar issues in the future.

14. Document Your Progress:

Keep records of your progress reviews, achievements, and adjustments. This documentation can serve as a valuable reference and motivation tool.

15. Celebrate Milestones:

When you reach important milestones or checkpoints, take the time to celebrate your achievements. This can help maintain your enthusiasm and momentum.

16. Stay Flexible and Adaptable:

Remember that life is dynamic, and circumstances can change. Be flexible and willing to adapt your goals and strategies as needed.

Regularly monitoring your progress is essential for effective goal management. It ensures that you stay focused, maintain motivation, and have the flexibility to make necessary changes to achieve your objectives. By following this process, you can maximize your chances of success in reaching your goals.

CELEBRATE ACHIEVEMENTS:

Recognize and reward yourself for reaching milestones.

Celebrating achievements in the goal-setting process is a rewarding and motivating way to acknowledge your progress and stay motivated. Here's a process for celebrating your achievements effectively:

1. Define Your Milestones:

Break down your larger goals into smaller, measurable milestones or checkpoints. These milestones act as key points in your journey where you can celebrate your progress.

2. Set Milestone Celebrations:

Determine how you will celebrate each milestone. Decide on specific rewards or celebrations for reaching these checkpoints. These celebrations can vary in size and significance.

3. Choose Meaningful Rewards:

Select rewards or celebrations that resonate with you personally. Ensure that they align with your interests, values, and preferences. The more meaningful the reward, the more motivating it will be.

4. Document Your Achievements:

Keep a record of your achievements and milestones. Document your progress with notes, photos, or journal entries. This documentation serves as a tangible reminder of your accomplishments.

5. Share Your Success:

Share your achievements with friends, family, or a support network. Celebrating with loved ones who can share in your joy and offer congratulations can enhance the experience.

6. Plan the Celebration:

Plan how you will celebrate each milestone in advance. Decide whether it will be a simple and personal celebration or a larger event involving others. Consider logistics and timing.

7. Reflect on Your Journey:

Take time to reflect on your journey toward your goals. Consider the effort, determination, and growth you've experienced. Reflecting on your progress can deepen your sense of accomplishment.

8. Express Gratitude:

Express gratitude for the resources, support, and opportunities that contributed to your success. Gratitude can enhance your overall well-being and add depth to your celebrations.

9. Treat Yourself:

Treat yourself to something special as a reward for your hard work and achievement. It could be a spa day, a favorite meal, a new book, or any indulgence that brings you happiness.

10. Organize a Celebration Event:

For significant achievements or the completion of a major goal, consider organizing a celebration event with friends and family. This can be a party, a dinner, or any gathering that honors your success.

11. Share Your Journey:

Share your progress and the story of your achievement with others. It can be inspiring to others and reinforce your own sense of accomplishment.

12. Practice Self-Compassion:

Be kind to yourself throughout the celebration process. Acknowledge that setbacks and challenges are part of any journey, and your resilience in overcoming them is worthy of celebration.

13. Use Celebrations as Motivation:

Let your celebrations serve as motivation for future goals. The positive reinforcement of celebrating achievements can inspire you to set and pursue new objectives.

14. Celebrate Others' Achievements:

Celebrate the achievements of those around you. Supporting and celebrating others can create a positive and motivating environment.

15. Give Back:

Consider using your achievements as an opportunity to give back to your community or a cause you care about. Celebrate by making a positive impact on others.

16. Maintain Perspective:

Remember that celebrating achievements is not just about the outcome but also about recognizing the effort and progress you've made. The journey itself is valuable.

By following this process, you can make the celebration of your achievements an integral part of your goal-setting journey. Celebrating milestones, no matter how small, can boost your self-esteem, keep you motivated, and add enjoyment and fulfillment to your pursuit of success.

The goal-setting process involves a series of steps designed to help you define, plan, and achieve your objectives effectively. Following a structured process can increase the likelihood of success. Here's a step-by-step guide to the goal-setting process:

IDENTIFY YOUR GOALS:

Start by identifying what you want to achieve. Your goals can be related to various aspects of life, such as career, personal development, health, finances, or relationships.

Make a list of your goals, both short-term and long-term. These can range from immediate tasks to aspirations that might take years to accomplish.

Identifying your goals is the foundational step in the goal-setting process. To identify your goals effectively, follow this process:

1. Self-Reflection:

Begin by taking time for introspection. Reflect on various aspects of your life, including your values, passions, interests, and long-term aspirations. Consider what truly matters to you.

2. Prioritize Areas of Focus:

Identify the key areas of your life where you want to set goals. These areas may include:

- Career and professional development
- Personal growth and development
- Health and fitness
- Relationships (family, friends, romantic)
- Finances and wealth building
- Education and skill acquisition
- Leisure, hobbies, and creative pursuits
- Contribution to society or community

3. Set Specific Goals Within Each Area:

Within each area of focus, set specific and meaningful goals. Use the SMART criteria (Specific, Measurable, Achievable, Relevant, and Time-bound) to create well-defined goals.

4. Ask Yourself Key Questions:

To refine your goals, ask yourself these questions:

- What do I want to achieve in this area?
- Why is this goal important to me?
- What is the desired outcome or result?
- How will I measure my progress and success?
- Is the goal realistic and achievable?

5. Consider Short-Term and Long-Term Goals:

Distinguish between short-term goals (achievable in weeks or months) and long-term goals (achievable in years). Both types of goals are important for personal growth and development.

6. Create a Goal Statement:

Craft a clear and concise statement for each goal that includes the specific objective, the deadline, and why it matters to you. This statement serves as a powerful reminder of your goals.

7. Organize and Prioritize:

Organize your goals into categories or areas of life. Prioritize them based on their importance and alignment with your values and long-term vision.

8. Ensure Balance:

Ensure that your goals cover a balanced spectrum of areas in your life. Strive for balance between personal, professional, health, and relationship-related goals.

9. Make Goals Challenging but Attainable:

While setting goals, aim for a mix of challenging goals that push you outside your comfort zone and attainable goals that boost your confidence and motivation.

10. Visualize Success:

Spend time visualizing what success would look like for each goal. This mental imagery can enhance your motivation and commitment.

11. Write Down Your Goals:

Document your goals in a written format. Whether you use a notebook, digital document, or a goal-setting app, writing them down reinforces your commitment and helps you track progress.

12. Share Your Goals (Optional):

If you're comfortable, share your goals with a trusted friend, family member, mentor, or coach. Sharing your goals can provide accountability and support.

13. Review and Revise:

Periodically review your goals to ensure they remain relevant and aligned with your values. Revise them as needed based on changing circumstances and priorities.

14. Take Action:

Begin taking action on your goals immediately. Break them down into actionable steps and start making progress.

15. Celebrate Achievements:

Celebrate your achievements along the way, no matter how small. Acknowledging your successes can boost motivation and maintain a positive attitude.

Remember that goal setting is an ongoing process. As you achieve goals, you can set new ones to continue your personal growth and development. Regularly revisit and refine your goals to ensure they align with your evolving values and aspirations.

MAKE YOUR GOALS SMART:

Refine your goals using the SMART criteria:

Specific:

Clearly define the goal in precise terms. What do you want to achieve, and why is it important?

Measurable:

Determine how you will measure your progress and know when you've achieved the goal.

Achievable:

Ensure that the goal is realistic and attainable given your resources, skills, and constraints.

Relevant:

Align the goal with your values, long-term objectives, and overall mission in life.

Time-Bound:

Set a specific deadline or timeframe for achieving the goal.

BREAK DOWN YOUR GOALS:

Divide larger, more complex goals into smaller, manageable steps or sub-goals. This makes the process less overwhelming and allows for steady progress.

Breaking down goals is a crucial step in goal setting, especially when you have larger or more complex objectives. Breaking them into smaller, manageable parts makes them less overwhelming and more achievable. Here's a process for breaking down your goals effectively:

1. Start with a Clear Goal:

Begin with a well-defined and specific goal. Make sure it follows the SMART criteria (Specific, Measurable, Achievable, Relevant, and Time-bound).

2. Identify the Key Components:

Analyze your main goal and identify the key components or sub-objectives necessary to achieve it. Think about what needs to happen to make your goal a reality.

3. Create Milestones:

Divide your goal into smaller milestones or stages. These are significant checkpoints along the way that will help you measure your progress.

4. Determine Action Steps:

Break down each milestone further into actionable steps or tasks. These are the specific actions you need to take to reach each milestone.

5. Prioritize and Sequence:

Organize your action steps in a logical sequence or order. Some tasks may need to be completed before others can begin.

6. Set Deadlines:

Assign deadlines to each milestone and action step. Be realistic about the time required for each task.

7. Allocate Resources:

Determine what resources you'll need for each task, such as time, money, tools, or assistance from others.

8. Monitor and Adjust:

Regularly monitor your progress toward each milestone and make adjustments as needed. If you encounter unexpected challenges or changes in circumstances, be prepared to adapt your plan.

9. Stay Accountable:

Hold yourself accountable for completing each action step by its deadline. You can use tools like to-do lists, project management apps, or calendars to help you stay on track.

10. Celebrate Achievements:

Celebrate your successes as you reach each milestone. Recognizing your progress can boost motivation and maintain a positive attitude.

EXAMPLE: BREAKDOWN OF A CAREER GOAL:

Main Goal: "Secure a promotion to a management position within my current company within the next two years."

Key Components:

- Enhance leadership skills.
- Demonstrate increased responsibility.
- Build a strong professional network.
- Showcase achievements and contributions.

Milestones:

- Complete a leadership training program.
- Successfully lead a cross-functional project.
- Attend industry conferences and networking events.
- Prepare and present a proposal for a new initiative.

Action Steps for Milestone 1 - Leadership Training:

- Research available leadership programs.
- Enroll in a relevant leadership course.
- Attend all sessions and complete assignments.
- Apply new leadership skills in the workplace.

Action Steps for Milestone 2 - Leading a Project:

- Identify a suitable project within the company.
- Propose to lead the project to your supervisor.
- Assemble a project team.
- Develop a project plan and timeline.
- Execute the project, managing tasks and team members effectively.
- Present the project results to senior management.

Action Steps for Milestone 3 - Networking:

- Research upcoming industry conferences and events.
- Register for selected events and make necessary travel arrangements.
- Attend conferences and actively engage with industry professionals.
- Follow up with contacts and connect on professional social networks.

Action Steps for Milestone 4 - Proposal Presentation:

- Identify a relevant initiative or improvement opportunity within your department.
- Research and analyze the initiative thoroughly.
- Develop a detailed proposal for implementation.
- Schedule a presentation to senior management.
- Deliver a persuasive and well-prepared presentation.

By following this process, you can effectively break down your goals into manageable steps, making them more attainable and less overwhelming. This approach also provides a clear roadmap for your journey toward achieving your objectives.

Create an Action Plan:

Outline the specific actions, tasks, and strategies you need to follow to achieve each sub-goal. Consider what resources and support you'll need.

Creating an action plan is a crucial step in the goal-setting process. It's a detailed roadmap that outlines the specific steps and tasks you need to take to achieve your goals. Here's a step-by-step guide to creating an effective action plan:

1. Clarify Your Goals:

Ensure your goals are specific, measurable, achievable, relevant, and time-bound (SMART).

Identify the main goal you want to achieve.

2. Break It Down:

Divide your main goal into smaller, manageable sub-goals or milestones. This makes the goal less overwhelming.

3. List Key Tasks:

For each sub-goal or milestone, list the key tasks or actions that need to be completed. Be as specific as possible.

4. Prioritize Tasks:

Determine the order in which you should complete these tasks. Identify which tasks are time-sensitive or dependent on others.

5. Set Deadlines:

Assign deadlines to each task to create a sense of urgency and ensure timely completion.

6. Identify Resources:

Determine the resources and tools you need to accomplish each task. This could include materials, information, or support from others.

7. Allocate Time:

Estimate the time required for each task. Ensure that your time allocation is realistic and aligns with your schedule.

8. Assign Responsibility:

If you're working with a team or have support from others, assign responsibility for specific tasks. Clarify who is accountable for what.

9. Monitor Progress:

Establish a system to monitor and track your progress. This could involve regular check-ins, task lists, or project management tools.

10. Anticipate Challenges:

Identify potential obstacles or challenges that may arise during the process. Develop contingency plans for handling these challenges.

11. Seek Support:

If you need help or expertise in specific areas, reach out to mentors, colleagues, or professionals who can provide guidance or assistance.

12. Stay Flexible:

Be open to adjusting your action plan as you go along. Sometimes, unforeseen circumstances or opportunities may require modifications.

13. Take Action:

Start working on your tasks according to your plan. Focus on one task at a time, completing each before moving on to the next.

14. Review and Evaluate:

Periodically review your action plan to assess your progress and make adjustments if necessary. Celebrate your achievements along the way.

15. Stay Accountable:

Keep yourself and, if applicable, your team accountable for completing the tasks as scheduled. Regularly communicate with others involved.

16. Track Results:

Keep a record of your achievements and milestones. This will help you stay motivated and provide a sense of accomplishment.

17. Review and Adjust:

After reaching a sub-goal or milestone, review your action plan and make adjustments as needed for the next phase of your journey.

Creating a well-structured action plan is essential for turning your goals into a reality. It provides a roadmap, keeps you focused, and ensures that you remain on track to achieve your objectives. Adjust and refine your action plan as needed to adapt to changing circumstances and stay committed to your goals.

Set Deadlines:

Assign deadlines or target dates for completing each step and achieving your goals. Having a timeline helps you stay focused and accountable

Setting deadlines is a critical component of effective goal setting. Deadlines create a sense of urgency and help you stay focused on accomplishing your goals within a specific timeframe. Here's how to set deadlines in the goal-setting process:

Make Your Goals Time-Bound (T) - SMART Goals:

Ensure that your goals are time-bound as per the SMART criteria. This means defining a specific date by which you intend to achieve your goal.

Specify a Completion Date:

For each of your goals, identify a clear and specific completion or achievement date. This date should be realistic and achievable but also challenging enough to motivate you.

Consider Short-Term and Long-Term Deadlines:

Depending on the nature of your goal, consider setting short-term and long-term deadlines. Short-term deadlines can help you track progress, while long-term deadlines are essential for overarching objectives.

Break Down Complex Goals:

If your goal is complex or involves multiple steps, break it down into smaller, more manageable tasks and assign deadlines to each task. This makes the goal more achievable.

Be Realistic:

Ensure that your deadlines are realistic and attainable. Consider your current commitments, available resources, and the complexity of the goal. Unrealistic deadlines can lead to frustration and failure.

Prioritize Tasks:

When setting deadlines for individual tasks related to your goal, prioritize them based on their importance and the sequence in which they need to be completed.

Account for Contingencies:

Anticipate potential obstacles and challenges that might cause delays. Build in some buffer time in your deadlines to account for unexpected setbacks.

Use a Calendar or Planner:

Use a calendar, planner, or digital tools to document your deadlines and keep track of your progress. This will help you stay organized and ensure you don't miss important dates.

Regularly Review Deadlines:

Periodically review and reassess your deadlines. If you find that a deadline is too ambitious or too lenient, adjust it accordingly.

Commit to Deadlines:

Make a personal commitment to meet your deadlines. Treat them with the same level of importance as any other appointments or obligations.

Seek Accountability:

Share your deadlines with a trusted friend, family member, or colleague who can help hold you accountable for meeting them.

Celebrate Milestones:

When you meet a deadline or reach a milestone on your path to achieving your goal, celebrate your achievements. This can provide motivation for continued progress.

Learn from Missed Deadlines:

If you miss a deadline, don't be discouraged. Instead, use it as an opportunity to learn from the experience and adjust your approach for future deadlines.

Setting deadlines is a practical and motivational technique for turning your goals into actionable plans. It helps you stay on track, prioritize tasks, and measure your progress. By adhering to your deadlines, you increase your chances of successfully achieving your goals.

Prioritize Your Goals:

Evaluate the importance and urgency of each goal. Focus on the goals that are most meaningful and relevant to your current circumstances.

Prioritizing your goals is an essential step in the goal-setting process. When you have multiple goals, it's important to determine which ones are most important and should be tackled first. Here's how to prioritize your goals effectively:

Review Your Goals:

Start by reviewing all the goals you've set. Make sure they are specific, measurable, achievable, relevant, and time-bound (SMART).

Categorize Your Goals:

Group your goals into different categories or areas of your life, such as career, personal development, health, relationships, or finance. This will help you see where your goals align.

Consider Your Values:

Reflect on your core values and what matters most to you. Your values can guide you in prioritizing goals that align with what you hold dear.

Set Long-Term and Short-Term Goals:

Distinguish between long-term goals (those you want to achieve in the future) and short-term goals (those you want to achieve soon). Prioritize one over the other, depending on your current circumstances.

Assess Impact and Significance:

Evaluate the impact and significance of each goal. Ask yourself, "How will achieving this goal improve my life or the lives of others?" Prioritize goals with greater positive impacts.

Consider Urgency:

Determine which goals have time-sensitive elements. Goals with imminent deadlines or immediate consequences may need to be addressed first.

Assess Feasibility:

Consider the feasibility of each goal. Goals that are realistic and attainable in your current situation should be prioritized over those that are less feasible.

Weight Your Goals:

Assign a priority or importance level to each goal, such as high, medium, or low. This can help you establish a clear hierarchy.

Use the Eisenhower Matrix:

The Eisenhower Matrix categorizes tasks or goals into four quadrants based on urgency and importance. Prioritize goals in the "Urgent and Important" quadrant first, followed by those in the "Important, but Not Urgent" quadrant.

Limit the Number of Priorities:

While you may have many goals, it's important to focus on a manageable number of top priorities. Having too many high-priority goals can lead to overwhelm.

Align Goals with Each Other:

Look for synergies between your goals. Sometimes, achieving one goal can make it easier to accomplish another. Aligning your goals strategically can enhance efficiency.

Revisit and Adjust:

Regularly revisit and adjust your priorities as circumstances change or as you make progress on your goals. What's a priority today may shift in the future.

Commit to Your Priorities:

Once you've identified your top priorities, commit to them. Allocate your time, energy, and resources accordingly, giving more attention to your highest-priority goals.

Communicate Your Priorities:

Share your priorities with those who need to be aware of them, such as your supervisor, team members, or loved ones. This ensures that everyone is on the same page.

Stay Focused:

Concentrate on your priorities and resist the temptation to become distracted by less important goals or tasks. Staying focused is key to achieving your top priorities.

Prioritizing your goals helps you concentrate your efforts on what matters most, increases your efficiency, and prevents you from spreading yourself too thin. By setting clear priorities, you can work towards achieving your most meaningful and impactful objectives.

Stay Committed:

Develop a strong commitment to your goals. Understand why you want to achieve them and remind yourself of these reasons regularly.

Monitor Progress:

Keep track of your progress by regularly reviewing your action plan and assessing how far you've come.

Use tools like calendars, to-do lists, or goal-tracking apps to help you stay organized.

Adapt and Adjust:

Be flexible in your approach. Circumstances may change, and you might need to adjust your goals or strategies accordingly.

Seek Support and Accountability:

Share your goals with friends, family, mentors, or colleagues who can provide encouragement and hold you accountable.

Join support groups or find a mentor or coach who can guide you in achieving your goals.

Celebrate Achievements:

Recognize and celebrate your accomplishments, both big and small. This reinforces your motivation and sense of achievement.

Review and Set New Goals:

Periodically review your goals to ensure they remain relevant. Once you've achieved a goal, consider setting new ones to continue your personal and professional growth.

Remember that the goal-setting process is iterative and ongoing. As you achieve one set of goals, you can use what you've learned to set and pursue new ones. Goal setting is a dynamic process that can help you continually improve and progress toward the life you envision.

PART 7

CHALLENGES OF GOAL SETTING

- Overambition: Setting unrealistic goals can lead to frustration and disappointment.

- Lack of Motivation: Without a compelling "why," it's easy to lose motivation.

- Lack of Planning: Insufficient planning can result in unclear steps and delays.

- Fear of Failure: The fear of not achieving a goal can deter some from setting them.

- Failure to Adapt: Not adjusting goals or strategies when circumstances change can hinder progress.

Effective goal setting is a skill that can be developed over time. It's essential to stay committed, stay adaptable, and continuously work toward your objectives.

While goal setting can be a highly effective strategy for personal and professional growth, it's important to acknowledge that it comes with its own set of challenges and potential pitfalls. Here are some common challenges of goal setting:

OVERAMBITION:

Setting overly ambitious or unrealistic goals can lead to frustration and disappointment. It's essential to strike a balance between setting challenging goals and ensuring they are achievable given your resources and constraints.

LACK OF MOTIVATION:

Without a compelling "why" or a strong sense of purpose behind your goals, you may struggle to stay motivated over the long term. It's crucial to have a deep and meaningful reason for pursuing your objectives.

LACK OF PLANNING:

Goals require careful planning and a well-thought-out action plan. Failure to plan adequately can result in unclear steps, inefficient efforts, and delays in achieving your goals.

PROCRASTINATION:

Procrastination can be a significant barrier to goal achievement. Putting off tasks and actions that are necessary to reach your goals can lead to missed deadlines and a lack of progress.

FEAR OF FAILURE:

The fear of not achieving your goals or the fear of making mistakes can be paralyzing. This fear can deter some people from setting goals altogether or cause them to abandon their goals prematurely.

LACK OF ACCOUNTABILITY:

If you keep your goals private and don't share them with others, you may lack external accountability. Sharing your goals with friends, family, or mentors can help keep you on track.

FAILURE TO ADAPT:

Circumstances can change, and sometimes your goals may become less relevant or feasible. Failing to adjust your goals or strategies in response to changing situations can hinder your progress.

SETTING TOO MANY GOALS:

Having too many goals at once can lead to overwhelm and scattered efforts. It's important to prioritize and focus on a manageable number of goals.

PERFECTIONISM:

Striving for perfection in pursuing your goals can be paralyzing. Accept that setbacks and imperfections are a natural part of the process, and don't let the pursuit of perfection hinder your progress.

BURNOUT:

An excessive focus on goals without considering your well-being can lead to burnout. It's crucial to maintain a healthy work-life balance and take care of your physical and mental health.

LACK OF FLEXIBILITY:

Being too rigid in pursuing your goals can lead to frustration. Sometimes, it's necessary to adjust your goals or strategies based on new information or changing circumstances.

COMPARING YOURSELF TO OTHERS:

Comparing your progress and success to others can be demotivating. Remember that everyone's journey is unique, and your goals should be tailored to your own values and aspirations.

EXTERNAL FACTORS:

External factors beyond your control, such as economic conditions, unforeseen events, or changes in circumstances, can affect your ability to achieve certain goals.

To overcome these challenges, it's essential to approach goal setting with a realistic mindset, seek support and accountability, maintain motivation through a strong sense of purpose, and be adaptable in your approach. Regularly reviewing and adjusting your goals as needed can help you stay on track and continue making progress toward your desired outcomes.

ABOUT THE AUTHOR

Arularase Baskar is a first-time author, certified trainer, and the visionary founder of KS Learning Edge Solutions. With a passion for education and personal development, Arularase has dedicated her career to empowering others to reach their full potential. Armed with a background in Sales And Marketing, she combines her expertise as a certified trainer with her natural gift for storytelling to create engaging and transformative learning experiences. Arularase debut book, "THE POWER OF PURPOSE," draws upon her years of experience and insights to offer practical strategies for achieving success and fulfillment in both personal and professional life.

AUTHOR'S WRITING STYLE:

Arularase's writing style is characterized by its clarity, warmth, and accessibility. As a certified trainer, she understands the importance of clear communication and engaging storytelling in facilitating learning and growth. Her writing seamlessly blends practical advice with inspirational anecdotes, making complex concepts relatable and actionable for readers of all backgrounds.

AUTHOR'S WORKS:

"THE POWER OF PURPOSE" marks Arularase's debut as an author, but her passion for empowering others extends beyond the pages of her first book. Through KS Learning Edge Solutions, she offers a range of training programs and workshops designed to help individuals and organizations thrive in today's rapidly changing world.

AUTHOR'S INSPIRATION:

Inspired by her own journey of personal growth and transformation, Arularase is passionate about sharing the tools and strategies that have helped her succeed with others. She believes in the power of lifelong learning and self-discovery, and strives to empower others to embrace their unique talents and passions.

ABOUT THE BOOK

"In 'THE POWER OF PURPOSE,' the author provides a comprehensive guide to effective goal setting, offering readers practical strategies to turn their aspirations into reality. The book delves into the importance of setting clear, measurable, and achievable goals, emphasizing the role of motivation and persistence in the journey towards success.

Readers will find valuable insights on overcoming obstacles, staying focused, and maintaining a positive mindset. Through real-life examples and actionable steps, the author demonstrates how anyone can create a roadmap for their dreams and navigate the challenges along the way. 'THE POWER OF PURPOSE' is not just a book; it's a roadmap for turning aspirations into attainable goals, inspiring readers to unlock their full potential and live a purpose-driven life."